D0910566

A HISTORY OF THE FRAGRANT ROSE

A HISTORY OF THE FRAGRANT ROSE

ALLEN PATERSON

This edition published in the United Kingdom in 2007
by Little Books Ltd, 48 Catherine Place, London SW1E 6HL

10 9 8 7 6 5 4 3 2 1

A CIP catalogue record for this book is available from the British Library.

ISBN 978 1 904435 75 4

Every attempt has been made to trace any copyright holders. The author and publisher will be grateful for any information that will assist them in keeping future editions up to date. Although all reasonable care has been taken in the preparation of this book, neither the publisher, editors nor the author can accept any liability for any consequences arising from the use thereof, or the information contained therein.

Printed and bound by William Clowes Ltd, Beccles, Suffolk

CONTENTS

List of Colour Illustrations

ACKNOWLEDGMENTS

An author's formal acknowledgments may seem a dry beginning to readers who, he hopes, are trying to get into the meat of the book. Without, however, the help I gratefully record, what follows would be more of a vegetarian repast.

My debt to Mr Graham Thomas is considerable. Not content with his own works on roses, he also nobly read the original typescript and made many valuable comments. Many people helped with sources and books. My thanks therefore go especially to my friends Derek Lucas and Godfrey Wace who pointed me to poems less commonly quoted; Miss Bridget Boland whose Shakespearean references were invaluable; to my friend Dr Edmund Launert of the British Museum (Natural History) for translation help; to Mr Jack Harkness and Dr Andrew Roberts (North East London Polytechnic) for advice on the x *Hulthemosa* hybrids.

As always, thanks to Mr Peter Stageman and Dr Brent Elliot of the Lindley Library for unfailing courtesy and help, and to Anne Stephenson for helpful research on my behalf.

I am most grateful also to growers, especially in America, who sent catalogues and information. Many gardeners in the UK and on the Continent welcomed my visits to whom I repeat my thanks, particularly to Mr Brian Hutchinson and Mr David Stone, Head Gardeners respectively of Castle Howard and Mottisfont Abbey; also to a posse of gendarmes at Bagatelle who let me in when the garden was closed.

Huge thanks must now go to Mr David Austin, not only for generously writing a foreword but, over the last twenty-five years, for introducing numbers of magnificent garden roses that combine the virtues of heritage roses with the best of modern types.

Finally a debt of gratitude to the team at Little Books who have brought life to this new edition of the *Fragrant Rose*.

Allen Paterson
Grovehill House

Foreword by David Austin

Many books on roses are published each year; far more than on any other flower. Many of these have very little to say that is new, although they are often beautiful productions – and each does its bit in the promotion of the rose. Allen Paterson's book, however, falls into quite a different category. Here we have a real classic of rose literature, beautifully written and full of interest.

The rose has, by far, the most extensive history of any flower. It seems to have the ability to always be present at the centre of civilisation over the centuries; all the way from the ancient civilisations of the Middle East, through Greek and Roman history and on through the whole of western history up to the present day. There can be no other garden flower that can rival it in this respect.

The rose is also one of the most beautiful of flowers; capable of many moods and many different manifestations. All these aspects, of this best-loved of all flowers, are faithfully portrayed in this book.

No one, insofar as I am aware – and I must have read most rose books of any importance – has ever written so well or so completely on the history of the rose. Indeed, it would be a great shame if this book was ever allowed to go out of print.

Allen Paterson is a vastly experienced horticulturalist and a man of great erudition. He trained at the Cambridge University Botanic Garden and eventually became Director of the Chelsea Physic Garden. After a period in education, he became Director of the Royal Botanical Gardens, Ontario. He is an authority on trees and has a vast knowledge of horticulture, generally – and is obviously a great lover of the rose. He has written some twenty books on horticulture and I can think of no-one more suitable to write a book on the history of the rose.

David Austin
David Austin Roses®
2006

INTRODUCTION

The study of nature, as Jean-Jacques Rousseau wrote in 1782,

> abates the taste for frivolous amusements, prevents the tumults of the passions and provides the mind with a nourishment which is salutary by filling it with an object most worthy of its contemplations.[1]

The idealist would hold this to be true until it is remembered that the progress of knowledge is apt to be a product of the battle between the innovators and those of entrenched views. Plants, and especially flowers, have always epitomized the quieter virtues: perhaps this is why an understanding of their sexuality was so long delayed and why botany was thought so suitable a subject for study by unemancipated Victorian ladies.

Yet, among the cognoscenti, increasing knowledge of plants both in general and specifically was beset with arguments as rancorous as in any other branch of science or the arts. This is nowhere more true than in the study of roses. 'What a pother,' wrote Nicholas Culpeper, 'have authors made with Roses! What a racket have they kept!' This fine example of seventeenth-century pot-calling-the-kettle-black refers, no doubt, to the fact that, even then, the origins of roses were a subject of speculation and discussion. Without the advantages that modern microscopy has brought to the study of plant genetics, intelligent theorizing was the only way forward in any such inquiry into groups of plants. Even with such aids, however, the 'pother' and the 'racket' continue and this is enormously stimulating as new discoveries undermine established tenets or, more surprisingly, support theories long neglected.

Such an ebb and flow of interest and information can refer to most groups of plants – all have their own protagonists and there is always some botanist or gardener ripe for a love affair with the most apparently dreary genus – but with roses the situation is rather different. Like the Mediterranean, the tide is almost always in, and it has been for centuries.

This should not be a cause for surprise. As this book attempt to show, the rose exists at several levels. We see it throughout history as an epitome of beauty from the earliest recorded time. From Sumer, 5,000 years before the birth of Christ, a golden filigree rose has come down to us. There are associations with the afterworld in ancient Egypt; Alexandria was also noted for producing huge numbers of roses for the decoration of Ptolemaic banquets. The same use in classical Rome brought roses into such disrepute as the flower of licentiousness that it took all the rose's powers and a thousand years before it reached its full symbolic flowering in medieval Christian Mariolatry.

From then on, in religion, in painting and in literature, the western ethic, on both sides of the Atlantic Ocean, has maintained a thread, a rope of roses, which is interwoven into many aspects of civilized life. The rose appears in fable and myth, in poetry and prose, as food and as medicine. It is also, and above all, *grown* as a major part of garden decoration throughout the temperate world.

Hence it is odd to refer to 'the rose' in the singular. As a genus of wild shrubs which comprises over 100 distinct species, it contains extraordinary diversity. This should, perhaps, not be surprising when it is realized that there are wild roses spread across the northern hemisphere from China and Japan, along the Himalayan foothills into southern India, throughout Europe and North Africa, and across North America from Canada to New Mexico. All, however distinct or distinguished, are recognizably roses.

There is thus no lack of fine plants for gardeners to use, yet the story of garden roses is not based upon what could be called nature's profligacy but, to be exact, upon her care to fit each rose perfectly to its habitat, whether it be moist, warm – temperate jungle, arid steppe or cold mountainside. On the contrary, the thousands of garden roses, annually propagated by the million, have been derived from hardly more than a dozen original wild species.

The range now available, through accidental or intentional hybridization, chance mutation or careful selection, is dauntingly vast. The story which tries to trace this development from wildling to sophisticated cultivar is a complicated and by no means completed one. It is still being written in two directions at once. Further research tells us more about the ancestral forms and new breeding programmes constantly attempt to incorporate hitherto unused species.

Origins of the historic cultivars which have been cherished in gardens for centuries are particularly difficult to trace. While any rosarian must be grateful to the authorities who have been quoted in the following pages, it would be foolish to assume that theirs are the last words on the subject. No botanist would ever claim such omniscience; the story will continue,

Even if the exact parentage of some early roses is still in doubt, the differences, at least between the various groups, are often very apparent. An interesting line of inquiry is to consider why certain flower-types attained great popularity in their time, only to be utterly neglected a generation or two later. The rate at which new cultivars have been introduced has so accelerated since the early years of the last century that periods of popularity have proportionately decreased. So quickly have some types gone out of favour that they have been utterly lost (and their genetic potential wasted) before the wheel of fashion has had time to bring them again into popular appreciation.

Such is the situation with many 'old-fashioned' roses. Although the continued existence of really historic roses has perhaps never been in doubt – could England ever have let the York and Lancaster Rose disappear? – immense numbers of eighteenth- and nineteenth-century roses, to say nothing of those from the early part of this century, are lost without trace. Fortunately, however, the best are apt to survive.

Fashion is, of course, the key to this seemingly frenetic search for new roses. The wish to grow the rare, the different, is an ever-present but irresistible snare in gardening. Early garden roses were garden roses because of their difference from the common native wildlings. They were double, they were darker or paler in colour, or they were striped. And, with hindsight, it seems possible to recognize in each a reflection of its time. Perhaps we can see the formality of seventeenth-century Dutch gardens in the regular rosettes of what Gerard calls *Rosa hollandica sive batavica*, the frivolous yet fully intentional flounces of Mme de Pompadour in eighteenth-century Centifolias and the weight of Victorian plush in the heavy Hybrid Perpetuals which dominated the period. Rose historians of the future will find easy analogies in the strident colours of so many roses of our own age.

In spite of this, we are fortunate in living at a time when, although the search for new roses has in no way abated, there is diversity on a number of fronts. Modern rose breeders, who would be delighted if they were able to produce a gentian-blue Hybrid Tea, are concerned with more than colour. There are problems of habit, disease resistance and hardiness to be overcome. And that of scent: in spite of the assurance of those whose ageing olfactory powers have not kept up with their memories of golden times past, some modern roses have a scent to rival that of their predecessors.

The parallel virtue of our present age is the effort that has been put into recovering from old gardens, around cottage and castle alike, the fine old roses which have, sometimes, fortuitously survived. No less laboursome has been the research which has resurrected lost names and attached them, after a century or more, to their true owners.

The subject of old roses is one of great complexity in which the nonspecialist may be foolhardy to venture. In *Old-Fashioned Flowers* (1939), Sacheverell Sitwell recognized this and was helpfully disarming. The present author must subscribe to his words:

> This Chapter on Old-fashioned Roses is written in humility and diffidence. The old Rose amounts to an

> enormous literature in itself, and its enthusiasts are in wait round every corner ready equipped for argument and contradiction.

Fortunately, argument and contradiction are highly valuable activities when constructively used: the succeeding forty years have produced much valuable material which Sir Sacheverell could not then have known. Much more will follow the moment these pages have gone to press.

New facts are already flooding in: nomenclature is revised – for example, *R. rubrifolia* to *R. glauca* (but we can be comforted that nursery catalogues will keep the name we know long enough to see many of us out). Among garden roses the blurring of the edges of certain groups that began a century ago has gone so far that, following a recommendation of the World Federation of Rose Societies, the use of some familiar names is to be discontinued. The titles Hybrid Tea and Floribunda, for instance, are to be replaced by Large Flowered and Cluster Flowered: less ambiguous perhaps but sadly lacking in style. The new classification will no doubt in time become familiar; for the present it seems better to discuss roses under the names by which they are still widely known, and so the old group names are used in what follows.

[1] *Lettres Elementaires sur la Botanique a Madame de L.*, 1782

An idealized garden of the early seventeenth century; roses climb the treillage

Chapter 1

The Roses of the Ancients

In all ages and cultures man has sought perfection, that elusive state to which only human beings free of worldly stain can aspire. And often, as with the myth of Eden, man is described as abandoning this state through his own folly – only to be condemned to seek it for eternity.

The garden has become the natural image of paradise, and it is not surprising that certain plants should be seen to symbolize important characteristics of the Ideal Place – none more so than the rose. In the original garden, of course, the rose itself possessed a perfection since lost. In Eden, according to the poet Milton, the rose was thornless, its subsequent armour a result of man's iniquity. (In fact, as the great horticulturist E. A. Bowles pointed out, the rose has never left Eden as its 'thorns' are merely epidermal offshoots).

As with most myths, it is impossible to give a simple starting date for the legends surrounding this, the most potent of symbolic plants. Archaeology and artefact combine with legends written and unwritten to make a chain of rose lore linking the present to the distant past.

Rosarians today hold one end of this still-extending chain. And if it cannot be known who originally held the other, it can be truthfully said that all Indo-European cultures have added their bead to this rosary.

Surprisingly, even the origin of the word 'rose' is mysteriously uncertain, though this does not prevent strong statements of apparent fact being made regularly in the literature. One derivation seems clear and is from the Greek *rhodon* (hence rhododendron: 'rose-tree'), this word being related to *rhein* meaning 'to flow'; the suggestion is that the scent of roses hangs upon the air until the wind causes it to stream away. Another Greek connection is with *rota*, a wheel, from the regular five-sided shape of the flowers. Rose as a name is immediately recognizable in most languages of German or Latin origin. With time the association has become irreversibly linked with the colour of the rose itself, just as so many other flowers give their names to provide a word by which they can be both described and referred to: lavender, violet, lilac, buttercup, primrose.

The mythological connection between other worlds and plants is as ancient as man. Birds, beasts and plants became the attributes of the divinities and we see, for example, the remains in Pharaonic Egypt of how 'animalocentric' religion, and hence life, became. The gods bore the visual likenesses of animals, which in turn were invariably related to specific plants. The rose, by becoming the flower of many gods or objects or worship, developed an aura of being itself worthy of similar veneration.

Although we are bound to refer especially to the myths of Greece and Rome upon which so many later stories are based, records of roses used as a *leitmotif* in the visual arts have by good chance come down to us from earlier ages still. Excavations of a 5,000-year-old Sumerian site have produced a rose bush with a ram standing in it, all of gold. (So interrelated are these symbols that one immediately thinks of the ram which, caught in a bush, was sacrificed in place of Isaac, and also of the unconsumed Burning Bush with the angel inside it which Moses saw.)

A thousand years before the classical period of Greece, the Minoan palace walls at Knossos were frescoed with beasts, fish and flowers, among which a six-petalled rose – with utterly typical leaves – is prominent. The rose motif is also seen in Minoan jewellery.

In classical myths the rose is the flower of Venus; its five petals correspond to the five points of the star of Venus or, in another of her guises, Aphrodite, goddess of love. Associations with love and romance come thick and fast (and is it purely chance that 'rose' is an anagram of

Eros?). The number five, of which rose flowers are built up, is symbolic in the Pythagorean tradition of *Hieros Gamos*, the sacred marriage between heaven and earth. Hence it was used to symbolize union in general. The stories credit roses both with being present at the birth of Venus – as Botticelli's famous painting shows – and also with being created by the same goddess.

An early account (Anacreon, *Ode* 51) of the fifth century BC runs thus:

> When the sea, from its foaming waves, created the beautiful, dew-sparkling Venus to carry her on its crests, when from Jupiter's brain Pallas emerged in full armour, the Earth, a new masterpiece of nature. Eager to hasten its unfolding, the Gods watered it with nectar and soon there rose up, majestically on her thorny column, this immortal flower.

And again:

> The rose is the Perfume of the Gods,
> The Joy of Men;
> It adorns the graces at the blossoming of Love,
> It is the favoured flower of Venus.

But, as with all ideas of perfection, the joy is the more ecstatic for the pain, the perfection is the more remarkable because of the sin. Venus again, hurrying to keep tryst with the irresistible Adonis, trod on a thorn. Her drops of blood sprang up as red roses. Bion (*Adonidis Epitaphium*, Idyll I) goes further with the same characters. Adonis is killed by a wild boar sent by the jealous Mars: 'Disaster, disaster, oh Venus, the beautiful Adonis is no more.' Hence it is the copious blood of Adonis (the colour of *Adonis aestivum* in spring fields of modern Greece) which grows into red roses while Venus' tears become white wood anemones. Elizabeth Barrett Browning puts the legend into verse in 'A Lament for Adonis' (Cytherea is another name for Venus/Aphrodite):

> Ah, ah, Cytherea's Adonis is dead.
> She wept tear after tear with the blood which was shed
> and both turned into flowers for the earth's garden-close,
> Her tears, to the wind-flowers; his blood to the rose.

Elsewhere Venus' tears produce white roses. Variations on the Venus/Adonis legend are legion but most encompass the rose in some form or other. In the next Olympic generation, almost inevitably Venus' son Amour or Eros becomes tangled with roses: he hides in them, is beaten with them. The result is that Eros becomes the prototype of all rosy *putti* in paintings or for decorating buildings both sacred and profane from that day to this.

Robert Herrick constructs his own myth on the origin of red and white roses in a verse to his current mistress, using Sappho instead of the more frequent

Amaryllis or Fair Phyllis as a *nom d'amour*. Doubtless he knew the real Sappho's 'Ode to the Rose, the Queen of Flowers'. Here is Herrick:

> Roses at first were white
> Till they co'd not agree
> Whether my Sappho's breast
> Or they more white sho'd be.
> But being vanquisht quite
> A blush their cheecks bespread,
> Since which (believe the rest)
> The Roses first came red.

The rose, dual symbol of joy and pain, has associations also with Dionysus the slain god. Garlands of roses were used by initiates at Dionysian festivals and at the altars of other gods, especially at those of Isis to whom the rose was also sacred. It seems that at the time that Apuleius wrote *The Golden Ass* in the second century AD, Rome was reacting against a period of religious scepticism in which the original pantheon of gods continued to have its role in story-telling, bawdy or not, but was now aided by an influx of oriental and Egyptian ideas brought into the old theology: hence Isis rather than Venus. It will be remembered that the hero (or autobiographical anti-hero) Lucius, because of his life of sinful excess, is turned into an ass, in which guise he survives a range of more or less unpleasant (if amusing) experiences.

But eventually Isis manifests herself to him in a dream and he is told that if on waking he browses on the garlands of roses left at the temple altar he will be returned to human form. The cure works, and though it is not the first instance of the medicinal effects of roses, it is perhaps one of the most dramatic.

A further legend, though centred upon the Olympian deities, is still current in the phrase *sub rosa* as a symbol of secrecy. In state papers of Henry VIII a letter of 1546 to Stephen Vaughan from Sir Robert Dymoke includes the passage:

> The sayde questyons were asked with lysence, and that yt should remayn so under the rosse, that is to say, to remayn under the bourde, and no more to be rehersyd.

Nearer our own time in the United States, John Adams, the second president, says in his *Familiar Letters* (1826):

> In Congress we are bound to Secrecy, but, under the rose, I believe that ten thousand men will be maintained in Massachusetts.

The phrase is explained thus by an anonymous Latin poet:

> The Rose is the flower of Venus and in order that his deeds may be hidden, Love (Eros) dedicated this gift of his mother to Harpocrates, the God of Silence. Hence

> the host hangs the rose over his friendly tables in order that his guests may know what is said beneath it will be regarded as secret.

Later, roses were carved as decorations on the ceilings of council chambers and confessionals with the same significance. The implication here of course is that Harpocrates should not tell tales about Venus' only too busy love-life.

Clearly roses were grown throughout the civilized world (which meant, to a Roman at least, within the Roman Empire), wherever it was at all possible to have a garden.

The catastrophe of the great Vesuvian eruption of AD 79, which overwhelmed Herculaneum and Pompeii, has proved invaluable to our knowledge of provincial Roman towns, houses and gardens. These last, as with town gardens today, were restricted in size and had high surrounding walls to screen them from other buildings. Layout was perforce formal, but in the flower beds that often surrounded a central pool grew roses, among other fashionable ornamentals. Presumably they were also trained up the columns of the peristyle – that loggia which bounded one or more sides of the garden. Often, too, in order to give a feeling of greater space, end walls were painted with *trompe l'oeil* scenes of the countryside seen through arbours of foliage and flowers. What better than the rose for this?

Authorities differ as to exactly which roses constituted those most grown. What is easy to discover – assuming that the distribution of the wild species has not altered much in the intervening two millennia, a very short time in the history of plant movement – is the very considerable number of species native to that vast empire. As this comprised by the early second century AD forty-three provinces stretching from Scotland in the North to Egypt in the south and from Tangier's Atlantic shore to the borders of the Caspian Sea, the geographical spread of perhaps fifty rose species is encompassed. Of these Dioscorides, in his medical treatise, refers to two: *R. sempervirens* (the identification is that of Charles Daubeny) and *R. foetida*. But in ancient Rome, as now, what made the highest price were flowers that were different. And doubling is different. Before the birth of Christ, Herodotus and Theophrastus in the fifth and third centuries respectively had described roses which possessed up to 100 petals. These mutant forms in which stamens had become petaloid have been generally taken to be selections of what, because of its double flowers, Linnaeus named (indeed Theophrastus and Pliny had already coined the binomial) *R. centifolia*, the 100-petal rose.

Certainly a double rose decorated Roman feasts and carnivals, but modern research has shown that this could not have been Linnaeus' *R. centifolia* (see page 91). It turns out in fact to be the Autumn Damask Rose

(*R. x bifera*). It is this rose too which is depicted in the Pompeian wall paintings mentioned above. In his *Georgics*, Virgil in the first century BC eulogizes the roses of Paestum, where the famous temple of the Hera still stands a few miles south of Pompeii. The description, '*Biferque Rosaria Paesti*' refers to their twice-a-year flowering habit and also explains the now accepted name, *R.* x *bifera*.

A pleasant conceit after a meal was to arrange for rose petals to fall from the ceiling: it is said that the bizarre Emperor Heliogabalus, almost two centuries later, took this to such excess that several guests became completely buried and were suffocated.

That roses became the hallmark of extravagance and licentiousness in the Roman world explains why they were avoided by the early Christian Church. Though not Christian, moral philosophers such as Seneca, who was Nero's tutor, rebuked current attitudes with the story of Smyrndiride the Sybarite who, like the later fairy-tale princess with the pea, was unable to sleep because, in his case, one of the rose petals in his bed was curled.

The Roman Empire spanned 1,000 years, but never had a monopoly on rose cultivation. Within and beyond its boundaries, cultures both free and subject added their part to the romance of the rose. Four hundred years before Caesar and Mark Antony fell in love with Cleopatra, Egyptians were using roses as decorative motifs, as had the Minoans before them. Wall frescoes and patterned cloth have come down to us. Usually the species that formed the pattern can only be guessed at, but the pure dry air of the desert that has preserved so much of ancient Egypt's past has also preserved in tombs an identifiable rose. This is *R. richardii*, the Holy Rose from Abyssinia. It appears that this particular plant had direct associations with death, as garlands of this flower, and only this, have been found among the grave-goods in Egyptian tombs of the first five centuries of the Christian era. *R. richardii* is a low, spreading bush, about the size of the Scots Burnet, with heads of pale pink flowers: it appears to be either a natural hybrid between *R. gallica* and *R. phoenicea* or a geographical variant of the former. If the hybrid status is correct, however, no definite explanation is available as to how the Syrian *R. phoenicea* contributed its part, though it is, incidentally, with *R. gallica,* present in the Summer Damask Rose. (Recent changes in nomenclature insist that *R. richardii* loses specific status and become synonymous with *R.* x *damascena.*) Perhaps this is the rose referred to in the third book of Maccabees, where the Egyptian city of Ptolomais is described as 'rose-bearing'.

The Judaic culture of the Old Testament, which overlaps those of Egypt and much of Rome, contains several references to roses. But translation is inevitably a difficulty. Did that English word which we read as rose, coming via Latin, Greek and Hebrew, begin in the mind of the writer of Isaiah or the 'Song of Solomon' as a rose?

The answer must be no.

A well-known passage from Isaiah, as translated in the King James Bible, runs:

> The wilderness and the solitary place shall be glad for them, and the desert shall rejoice and blossom as the rose.

The Jerusalem Bible, however, renders that same verse thus:

> Let the wilderness and dryland exalt
> let the wasteland rejoice and bloom
> let it bring forth flowers like the jonquil
> let us rejoice and sing for joy.

Clearly Isaiah's words, dating perhaps from 700 years before the birth of Christ, are concerned with prophetic message and not with botanical veracity. The Jerusalem Bible's substitution of jonquil certainly makes more sense from that point of view: in so many areas of the eastern Mediterranean littoral the winter rains herald at around Christmas time sheets of the lovely scented *Narcissus tazetta* springing up from under rocks and in the most unlikely soil. The rose is used symbolically to represent the beautiful and perfect – an ideal rather than a reality.

The same context must be seen in the oft-quoted lines from the 'Song of Songs'. This is in the dialogue of the bride and bridegroom:

I am the rose of Sharon
the lily of the Valleys.
As is a lily among the thistles
So is my love among the maidens.

Rose here, it is suggested, is used as a name, or as a concept which is symbolic of spring, rather than as an actual flower; if one looks, as most commentators have done, for what the 'Song of Songs' actually meant, a number of spring flowers of the Palestine hills are possible. Most – Adonis, Narcissus, Crocus, Colchicum and so on – have had their advocates. It is a matter which will probably never be settled. In the 'Song of Songs' several plants are used to exemplify beauty, goodness or desirability: apples, cedar, cypress, vines, henna-flowers, myrrh, all occur, and the rose is but another. Needless to say, plants to which the vernacular name Rose of Sharon is now attached, from *Hibiscus syriacus* (native of India and China) to *Hypericum calycinum* (native of European Turkey, northern Anatolia and Bulgaria), have no claim to it whatsoever in terms of the Biblical origin of the phrase.

Nonetheless there is no lack of true rose species native to the eastern shores of the Mediterranean: there are several pink dog-rose types from *R. canina* itself to *R. collina* and *R. glutinosa*, as well as the classic yellows, *R. foetida* (the Austrian briar) and *R. rapinii*, the wild single form of the now rare and difficult *R. hemisphaerica*. This latter plant has, however, been suggested as a common rose in Asia Minor in early times. Perhaps this was the plant grown in a rose bed in Jerusalem where, according to an old Mithraic tradition dating from the time of the ancient prophets, no other garden was allowed.

Jewish legend associates pink roses symbolically with Paradise. Dawn, it is said, is the reflection of the roses of heaven just as the glow of sunset reflects the flames of hell. For the Jews, eight hundred roses were reputed to adorn the tent of each pious man in heaven.

It is interesting to note the development of a parallel here with the stigma of luxury and libertinism which roses acquired in Roman times. Rose oil was very much, because of its cost, a material restricted to the upper classes, though the actual rose flower, together with myrtle, formed part of every bridegroom's garland. In the 'Book of Wisdom' (2.8) we read (Jerusalem Bible translation):

> Come then let us enjoy what good things there are; use this creation with the zest of youth: take our fill of the dearest wines and perfumes, let not one flower of springtime pass us by. Before they wither crown ourselves with roses.

It is not surprising that of this verse only the last phrase is generally quoted: recommendations of such Dionysiac goings-on are not likely to be considered suitable.

Predating Heliogabalus, the Holy Raba brought a gift to a Persian satrap whom he found sitting up to his neck in roses. The satrap asked 'Have ye aught like this in Paradise?' (An alternative version reports the satrap merely in his bath heavily scented with rose oil: a more likely but less attractive picture.)

Since roses have been admired and used as motifs in art from the dawn of civilization it is no surprise that each culture has developed its own rose lore. While much is clearly derivative, some seems to have been engendered *de novo* from direct observation of the beauty of the flower itself. Everywhere roses are either the product or the begetters of perfection. From opposite sides of the northern hemisphere come the following two legends.

> The Turks after much deliberation concluded that the rose, as well as rice, was formed from the sweat of the prophet Mahomet. This is the reason why Mahomedans show such veneration for the rose. If they find a rose lying on the ground, they hasten to gather it up. And having kissed it they insert it in some crevice in a wall, as if to protect such a precious flower from defilement.

This story takes place in the centre of inherited rhodophilia, yet the legend of the origin of the American Cherokee Rose (*R. laevigata*) (as quoted by Peter Coats in his 'The Pageant of the Rose' from *Roses*) seems to have no antecedents:

> The Cherokee Indians were once led by a brave and handsome warrior whose name was Tuswenahi. One day, when this warrior returned from a hunting trip which took him far from home, he found his settlement destroyed and his sweetheart, Dowansa, missing. His frantic search for her was ended when the Nannshi, or little people, told him that in order to save her they had had to turn her into a white rose with golden breasts. The following spring found the maiden blooming in full purity, but she begged the little people to give her thorns to protect herself against thoughtless people, including Tuswenahi himself, her lover, who carelessly trampled on her flowers. So the Nannshi covered every stem with multitudinous prickles, so sharp that even animals do not dare to eat them.

Again and again such stories appear. Often they become extended and encapsulated in Christian mythology, as Christianity, on the pragmatic principle of joining what you cannot beat, ingested much of the folklore of its predecessors.

Yet, in spite of early references being predominantly legend, occasionally light breaks through to show that roses were actually grown (as indeed they must commonly have been for such a wealth of stories to have built up). It would be pleasant to imagine the terraces of those famous Hanging Gardens of Babylon, which were one of the seven wonders of the ancient world, to have been festooned with cascades of the rose species which the Babylonian empire could have called upon. But alas no planting plan nor plant list exists, if there ever had been one.

However, there is a definite record of the rose garden possessed by King Midas of Phrygia in Macedonia, written by the Greek historian Herodotus around 500 BC. Again, very little detail exists to inform us about what must have been, in classical times, a very important commercial rose-growing industry. You cannot wade in roses eighteen inches deep, like Antony and Cleopatra, or drown people in rose petals like Heliogabalus, without there being a very considerable supply. Presumably this supply was highly seasonal. Europe had normal home-grown flowers in May and June plus the September flush from the Autumn Damask, but the supply was extended by winter imports from Egypt, with its milder climate and Nile-irrigated soil. There is a reference in Martial commenting that 'roses in winter bear the highest price' – surely, even then he was stating the obvious.

CHAPTER 2

ROSA MUNDI: ROSES IN THE MEDIEVAL WORLD

The spread of roses throughout western Europe owes much to the apparently inexorable advance of Islam. At the time, Islamic culture developed science, medicine and the arts to heights hitherto unattained. With the decline of the Roman Empire and its fall to tribes from the north and east, whose names, Goth and Vandal, are still synonymous with barbaric behaviour, Europe died as a centre of human culture. Pockets of past glory remained, but they had lost the will to combine and extend themselves. Now the vital youth of Islam came to move again the wheel of civilization.

As Arabs moved from Persia, which they had conquered by the seventh century AD, the flowers of the Middle East followed them, gathering up others in their train westward to Spain, much of which they took in the eighth century, and eastward to India two centuries later.

Having originated among the nomadic people of the desert in what had been the fertile crescent of Mesopotamia, the culture of Islam naturally (just as Jewish civilization had previously) developed the idea of a watered garden as the ideal of paradise. This was originally a Persian concept, from which language the very word paradise comes. Persian gardens, which continued with Islam, were places of quiet and of contemplation 'where a man composes his soul and is at one with his world'; each is 'the place of unification within and without'[1] and, it is suggested, each garden-paradise is the 'realization of the earth's potentiality.'

The re-creation of the garden-paradise ideal by the Moslems arrived at a peak of sophisticated perfection which can still be seen at the ends of Islam's earthly empire in the gardens of the Generalife and the Alhambra in Spain and in great Mogul gardens such as Shalamar and Nishat in present-day Kashmir (whose roses unfortunately are today conventional Hybrid Teas combined, in a not particularly aesthetic combination, with Tagetes, Zinnias and the 'malignant magenta' – in Gertrude Jekyll's deathless phrase – *Gomphrena globosa*.)

In the prime of Islam, the classic roses grew. According to Avicenna (AD980–1037), the famous Arab physician, a rose was widely cultivated in Syria for the manufacture of rosewater and for use in medicines. His description shows it to be that Roman commercial rose, of Paestum, *R.* x *bifera* or the rose Autumn Damask. By the twelfth century it was with the Arabs in Spain, though doubtless predating the extant reference by many years. Indeed the Romans in their colonies of Hispania and Baetica may well have grown it there 1,000 years before.

Not surprisingly, the Arabic poets used the rose, as had earlier writers from the Middle East, as the epitome of perfection, for in Persia, too, the rose had been considered the Queen of Flowers. But perfection, apparently, can be a snare. In the twelfth century the famed Persian poet, Nizami, tells a peculiar story:

> Of two rival physicians and a duel they fought, not with swords and daggers, but with poisons. First one caused the other to swallow a lethal pill, but was frustrated by the opponent immediately taking an antidote which transformed the pill into something as innocuous as a sweetmeat. Then it was the other's turn. Taking a rose, he appeared to cast a spell on it, and then asked the rival doctor to sniff it. No sooner had his opponent done so than he collapsed and died.

This Borgian use of that which is presumed to be both pure and perfect (not unlike the glossy poisoned apple proffered by the witch to Snow White) is paralleled in Jewish legend of about the same time as the Persian story. A famous cabbalist in Prague named Low, who was a favourite of King Rudolf II, died, it is related, through the perfume of a rose. The sage had led so blameless a life that only by assuming the form of the rose perfume itself was Death able to reach him.

The commonest connection between Islam and Christendom, between the mysterious East and the medieval western world is not, sadly, through such blameless activities as the cultivation of roses, but through the Crusades. These extraordinary expeditions, initially instigated to recapture the Holy Places from the Infidel, but invariably confused by the infighting of the Christian allies, often produced, for those knights who returned alive, mementoes of great value and romance. Tradition has it, for example, that the King of Navarre and Count of Champagne, Thibaut IV (known as *'le Chansonnier'*), brought back from the Crusade which he led in 1239–1240, the famous Apothecary's Rose.

This is *R. gallica officinalis*, which Thibaut introduced to Provins in the modern *département* of Seine et Marne. However doubtful that original attribution may be, it is a fact that Provins was the centre for the commercial culture of this medicinal rose for six centuries from Thibaut's time: what is possible is that the king, even if he did not himself import the rose, had the foresight to promote a very successful industry. The Apothecary's or Provins rose is a red semi-double flower and, surprisingly, can be considered with safety, through this Saracenic and French descent, to be the Red Rose of England.

The first recorded mention of it in England is by a monk of St Mary's Abbey, York in 1368: the 'red rose is ye badge of England and hath growne in that countrye for as long as ye mynde of man goeth'. It seems very probably that it was this rose that Edmund Crouchback, first Earl of Lancaster, brought back to England with him in 1279 and subsequently adopted as his emblem. Edmund, second son of Henry III of England and Eleanor of Provence, became by marriage to Thibaut's daughter-in-law (as her second husband), Count of Champagne. He consequently lived for some time at Provins, surrounded by *R. gallica officinalis.* Perhaps his adoption of it was a compliment to his wife, Blanche. Edmund's mother, Queen Eleanor, already used a white rose as her emblem and this descended to her eldest son Edward I. Hence, royal roses used as heraldic badges predate the Wars of the Roses by 200 years. As Parkinson wrote in 1629, but without saying when (in his *Paradisi in sole Paradisus Terrestris*), the white and the red rose were 'assumed by our precedent Kings of all others, to be cognisances of their dignities'.

Although recognizable heraldry made its first appearance in England during the second half of the eleventh century, it was not until the reign of Henry III (1216-1272) that it developed fully into the specialized system with its own language which those versed in such things would understand today. In early times, the wearing of emblems made clear a man's rank, his allegiance, and hence his likely behaviour. Those who bore arms, then as now, did so by inheritance or by award. Inevitably we associate heraldry less with its early actual uses than with a half-fictitious Sir Walter Scott-like world of jousting, chivalry and 'gentil parfit' knights. Doubtless the Crusades were in most cases as unpleasant as any other war but they clearly gave a fillip to heraldry and to the armigerous crusader.

The title page to John Parkinson's Paradisi in Sole Paradisus Terrestris

The devices painted upon shields or woven upon tabards and banners made up a pictorial and symbolic, often punning, language, their origins taken from a wide range of models. But the natural world was pre-eminent. Extraordinary bestiary creatures (as exemplified by the Queen's beasts) were frequent, as were many plants. By the time heraldry became both more common and more prestigious, the rose among other emblems had already been adopted by the English royal house. It is a flower which in the simplest single form lends itself well to broad representations recognized easily from a distance. Shown full-face the heraldic rose emerges much like a floral diagram of the *Rosaceae* in a late nineteenth-century botany textbook. Five lobed petals enclose raylike stamens which in turn surround the carpels. Between the petals the tips of the sepals show as five points.

The language of heraldry describes the variations in colour which make each basic emblem available to a number of people who are usually scions or branches (the language is apt for the rose) of the original stock. Hence, a *rose gules* is entirely red, while a *rose gules, seeded or barbed vert* has red petals, gold carpels and stamens and green tips to sepals. Such colouring is also described as *rose gules, barbed and seeded proper*, because the College of Heralds knows what colours a rose ought to be.

The *Rose en Soleil* or Rayed Rose shows a white heraldic rose, usually single, as the centre of a golden-rayed sun. This was a confection adopted by King Edward IV after his Yorkist victory at Mortimer's Cross in 1461. (The double form of the *Rose en Soleil* appears still upon the regimental colours of the 5th Company, the Grenadier Guards.) Shakespeare's lines from *Richard III*, with rose heraldry in mind, make added point:

Now is the winter of our discontent
Made glorious summer by the *sun* of York.

The Tudor rose is an heraldic device to combine the white rose of York with the red rose of Lancaster. Whereas in the thirteenth century, as emblems of Edward I and Edmund Crouchback, they were borne by brothers, a century later they were the property of related warring factions and hence gave the name to that bloody civil conflict which sounds so full of romance when called the Wars of the Roses.

Shakespeare dramatizes the opening quarrel, set in the garden of the Temple in London in *Henry VI, Part I*, in which white and red roses are purported for the very first time to be taken as Yorkist and Lancastrian emblems. Knowing that this is not true in no way detracts from the symbolic drama:

Plantagenet: Let him that is a true-born gentleman
And stands upon the honour of his birth,
If he suppose that I have pleaded truth,
From off this briar pluck a white rose with me.
Somerset: Let him that is no coward nor no flatterer
But dare maintain the party of the truth,
Pluck a red rose from off this thorn with me.

> *Warwick*: I love no colours, and, without all colour
> Of base insinuating flattery
> I pluck this white rose with Plantagenet.
> *Suffolk:* I pluck this red rose with young Somerset
> And say withal I think he held the right.

Years and battles later the roses were finally brought together again with the reign of Henry Tudor (1485-1509), the Lancastrian victor of the Wars. Having plucked the crown (in Shakespeare's highly Tudor-biased version) 'from the dead temples of this bloody wretch' (Richard III), Stanley gave it to Henry who in his final speech promises that:

> We will unite the white rose and the red:
> Smile Heaven upon this fair conjunction,
> That long hath frown'd upon their enmity.

The real dynastic conjunction, however, was Henry's politic marriage with Elizabeth of York, heiress of Edward IV and bearer of the white rose.

The heraldic combination shows a rose with two rows of petals; usually the big red outer petals enclose and surround, emphasizing the Lancastrian triumph, the inner whorl of white. Such roses adorn numbers of tombs or look down as bosses from church roofs where the vaulting groins meet.

It is interesting to note how the archaic language of heraldry not infrequently uses words that are still current among country people today, though otherwise lost. People still talk of 'taking off slips' from a plant when wanting to root cuttings. A slipped rose, or other plant, on a coat of arms shows not just the flower but a stem and often leaves as well. The Badge of England shows one and is described as 'A Tudor Rose barbed and seeded proper, stalked and leaved vert, ensigned with an Imperial Crown'. Similar badges may be seen as carved decoration in the various Chapels Royal. Captain H. S. Lecky (in *The Rose Annual* for 1931) hints of a prophylactic rather than a medicinal action of roses by noting that the three wives of Henry VIII who adopted the rose as part of their arms avoided the worst of his wrath. Catherine of Aragon (divorced) used a rose, a pomegranate and a sheaf of arrows; Jane Seymour (death by natural causes) had a phoenix rising from a castle with a Tudor Rose on either side; while Henry's widow, Catherine Parr, adopted a crowned maiden's head rising from a Tudor Rose.

That choice of colour and emblem was important to give meaning to a grant of arms is made clear by the letters patent of 14 January, 1448-1449 from King Henry VI to the new sister-foundation of Eton College, King's College, Cambridge.

> In a black field three silver roses, having a mind that our newly founded College enduring for ages to come, whose perpetuity we wish to be signified by the stability of the black colour, may bring forth the rightest

> flowers redolent in every kind of science to which also, that we might impart something of regal nobility, which might declare the work truly regal and famous, we have ordained to be placed in the chief of the shield parcels of the arms lawfully due to us in our Kingdom of England and France, partly of azure with a flower of the French and of gules with a gold leopard passant.

Perhaps it is not surprising that Henry Wise, gardener to Queen Anne, took as his badge when granted arms 'a demy-lion argent, holding a damask rose, stalked and seeded proper'. His even more celebrated contemporary who laid out Versailles for Louis XIV was more down to earth. On being offered a crest, Le Nôtre said he already had one: three slugs crowned with cabbage leaves.

In the sixteenth century only a Protestant monarch and an English one, who had her own dynastic reasons for making the claim, would presume to adopt as her motto and her badge *rosa sine spina* – the rose without thorns. Such a title, of course, truly belongs not to Queen Elizabeth I but to the Virgin Mary. While we see a continuum of rose symbolism from prehistoric times to the present, linking culture with culture, there is the inevitable gap of years between the rose's association with pagan Roman excess and its eventual reacceptance as the epitome of purity and perfection.

Eithne Wilkins in *The Rose Garden Game* (1969) has delved into rose symbolism more deeply than perhaps

Contratenor.

Canon fuga in diapatessaron.

℟. Surrexit dñs uere .
alla alla ℣. Et apparuit
simoni alla alla. Gloria p
Surrexit ℣. Surrexit do
minus de sepulcro. alla ℟
qui pro nobis pependit in
ligno alleluya.
Ad nonam Hymnus
Rerum deus
tenax uigor i
immotus in te
permanens lucis diurne
tempora successibus det
minas.
Largire clare uesperum
quo uita nusq̃ decidat s
premiũ mortis sacre perhennis
instet gloria.
Presta pater piissi
me. psalmus
Mirabilia testimo
nia tua: ideo scru
tata ẽ ea anima mea
Declaratio s̃monum
tuorum illuminat: et intel
lectum dat paruulis.
Os meum aperui et
attraxi spiritum. quia man
data tua desiderabam
Aspice in me et mise
rere mei secundum dilige
tium nomen tuum
Gressus meos dirige
s̃m eloquium tuum: et nõ
dñetur mei oĩs iniusticia:
Redime me a calum
niis hominum ut custodi
am mandata tua
Faciem tuam illumi
na super seruum tuũ: doce
me iustificationes tuas
Exitus aquarum de
duxerunt oculi mei: quia
non custodierunt legẽ tuã
Justus es. ps. Sade.
es domine: et rec
tũ iudiciũ tuum
Mandasti iusticiam te
stimonia tua et ueritatem
tuam nimis
Tabescere me fecit ze
lus meus: quia obliti st̃
uerba tua inimici mei
Ignitum eloquium
tuum uehementer: et seruus
tuus dilexit illud.

Maintenant est
droit que vo' die
La contenance
La jalousie
Qui est male suspection
Il ny eust ou pays macon
Ne pionnier quelle ne mande
Si leur fait faire et cōmande
Entre les rosiers des fossez
Qui cousteront deniers assez

Car ilz sont fausses et parfons
Dessus les bors font les macons
Vng mur de quarreaux biē tailliez
Bien appointez et habillez
Dont le fondement par mesure
Est assis sur roche tresdure
Jusque au pie du fosse descent
Et vient amont en estressant
Loeuvre en est plus forte dassez
Les murs furent si compassez

anyone and the next pages are greatly indebted to her book. In the Marian context she writes:

> Since the rose was already a pre-Christian symbol of beauty, love, wisdom and mystery, it is not surprising that it was from a very early time used as a symbol of the beautiful, wise and mysterious Virgin, Bride and Mother, Mary.

In the first half of the fifth century, the poet Sedulius combined that symbolic attribution with an enduring comparison:

> As blooms among the thorns the lovely rose, herself without a thorn,
> The glory of whose crown she is,
> So, springing from the root of Eve Mary the new Maiden
> Atoned for the sin of that first Maiden long ago.

The description of Mary as the new peerless Eve is often paired with that of Christ as the new Adam. Together they exist in the epitome of rose gardens, Paradise, the new Eden. Medieval commentators were not slow to use the analogy of the red petals of the rose with the spilt blood of Christ, just as it had been used by classical writers for other gods. Nor, as St Bernard points out, did they fail to recognize the Five Wounds of Christ on the

Cross in the pentamerous pattern of the flower. (Jesuit missionaries in South America used the five-petalled passion flower to good effect.) Medieval legends repeat, with alteration only to the protagonists or the place, the universal tales of the rose's origin. The first white and red roses appeared, it is said, to prove the innocence of a 'fayre mayden' who had been wrongly accused of crime and sentenced to be burned.

> She entered the fire and immediately the fire was extinguished and the faggots that were burning became red rose bushes full of roses and those that were unkindled became white rose bushes; and these are the first rose trees and roses both white and red, that ever any man saw.

Alternatively, and again at Bethlehem, Mary put out her veil to dry on a nearby rose bush which miraculously produced thereafter, not the red blossoms it had hitherto borne, but pure white flowers. This legend is from Germany; similar ones or further variants on the theme continue to appear throughout Christendom.

To the medieval mind the place where roses grew became itself both mysterious and holy. They were cultivated, more perhaps, by monkish illuminators of manuscripts and by painters than by gardeners. Roses clamber up trellises, they make bowers for the Madonna and her Child, they are held by angels and cherubim –

those Eros-figures of sacred art. Sometimes, as in the illustrations to the *Romaunt of the Rose*, the garden is sited within the enclosure of a castle's castellated walls; sometimes the roses bloom around a gazebo illogically sited in a flowery meadow. Knowing both something of horticulture and of the uncertain social conditions of the time, we must assume that the enclosed garden rather than the isolated gazebo existed in fact. Miss Wilkins logically suggests the gazebo picture to have oriental influence: so often in Persian miniatures the Shah sits in such a delicate building.

Rosary Sunday is celebrated by the Roman Catholic Church to commemorate the great Venetian victory at sea over the Turks at Lepanto in 1571. And in the Proper of the Mass for that Sunday the well-known words from the Book of Ecclesiastes (39.17) are used three times symbolically of the Virgin: '*Iquasi rosa plantata super rivos aquarum*' (like a rose planted beside the waters). In other services she is invoked as *Rosa Mystica*.

> Although the development began in the twelfth century, it was especially during the fourteenth and fifteenth centuries that the rose, rose bush, rose garden and rose garland were used, with almost monotonous persistence, in Marian symbolism … By the middle of the fifteenth century the concept 'rose garden' as also 'wreath of roses' was well established as symbolising devotion to the Mystic Rose, mother of the Divine

> Child, and the beads were becoming an accepted element in the whole complex.[2]

The words 'rosary' or 'rosarium' have extended their meanings from, firstly, that place where one grows roses to that of a book and subsequently, because of the sort of book, the string of beads which bears the name today. A thousand years and more encompass this change. In the Middle Ages a conceit developed for referring to books (which, it must be remembered were rare, expensive works, handwritten page by page with great beauty) as flower gardens. Rosarium or rose garden became an especially favoured name. Their contents were various but, whether sacred or concerned with Mariolatry or profane and associated with alchemy (where the rose is referred to as *flos sapientum* – the flower of those initiated into the mystery), their imagery clearly interrelates: love, wisdom, mystery, the search for perfection in body and soul, these were the concern of the rosaria. One of the first recorded, written by the physician Arnold of Villanova (*c.* 1285–1311), is called *Rosarium Philosophorum*, but gradually the term becomes reserved for paeans to the Virgin Mary. These, by 1400, were becoming organized, especially in monastic orders, into definite forms with a prescribed number of Aves, Paternosters and so on. Heinrich Egher of Kalkar, a leading Carthusian who died in Cologne in 1408, ordered that fifty Aves should make up a rosarium.

A current definition of the rosary is that of a set of devotions consisting of the recitation or chanting of the decades of Aves, each decade being preceded by a Paternoster and followed by Gloria. But why rosary? What has it to do with roses? Perhaps the foregoing paragraphs tell some of the story: an ordered collection of good and desirable things may be seen to be like a collection of perfect flowers – most flowers encapsulating the idea of other-wordly perfection because they cannot be made by man – and hence by analogy to be called after the Queen of Flowers itself.

The word, of course, is now more commonly used for the sequential *aide-mémoire* to the saying of a set of devotions. In this connection rosaries predate the Christian era by centuries. Chaplet strings of prayer beads were associated in India with the cult of Shiva, the creator and destroyer, and with his consort Kali. From India their use moved north and eastward to Tibet and China and eventually to Japan, where recognizable rosaries became a part of monkish equipment. From India, too, came the use of prayer beads by Persians and Arabs and their acceptance by Islam.

Many and various were the materials from which the beads of the rosary were made. Not often, though, do they bear any close relation to roses themselves. A very special exception, however, would seem to be the beads still made by the nuns of St Theresa of Avila's Carmelite convent at Avila in Spain. They are made of kneaded rose petals. It has been suggested that in those beleaguered monasteries where the flame of classical culture still burned, a few roses were grown both for their medicinal properties and for use as rosary beads.

Obviously, anything can make a rosary. But it was not until the end of the fifteenth century that its size became regularized and its invention formally attributed to St Dominic. Legend has it that Dominic was visited by the Virgin armed with a rosary which was to help him overcome the wicked heresy of Albigensianism.

The late fifteenth century saw an extraordinary burst of religious activity with Marian devotions to the fore. Already the term 'rosarium' with the older symbolism of rose garden was current to describe the prayers; now it began to refer to the beads themselves. Throughout Europe, city guilds of bead makers, and paternosters, proliferated, and street names – Paternoster Row in London and Via dei Coronari in Rome – still reflect this.

In the early Middle Ages, while it was tacitly accepted that the Virgin Mary was the most pure and perfect lady worthy of veneration and that all Christians looked to her for intercession, she was the more particular property – if the phrase can be used in this context – of the vocational religious and the monastic houses. In the world outside a parallel cult of chivalry developed in which the ideals of womanly purity and perfection were seen to adorn more accessible, though still physically untouchable, ladies. In this the rose takes a similarly symbolic place.

The concept of courtly love spread from Provence in the twelfth century through the agency of wandering troubadours whose songs, as with popular songs of any age before or since, concerned romantic relationships between men and women; life and lust. The troubadour's message, however, referred to very special people: the chivalrous knight and his chosen lady. Courtly love is, ostensibly at least, unrequited and refers to any lady except the protagonist's actual wife.[3] It is frequently, though not surprisingly, illustrated as taking place in a rose garden. Surrounded by the flower of love, the ideal lovers find an ideal tryst.

Much Islamic love-poetry has similar themes and, 'The Arab and Provençal movements are so closely contemporary that one need not press the question how far the Arab influence promoted the cult of courtly love'.

There is clearly much connection between this and developing Mariolatry for 'often the troubadour and the monk are barely distinguishable from one another, each dedicated to his Lady, composing songs for her, aspiring to be crowned with roses at her hands, or kneeling to offer her roses' .

Chivalry and heraldry unfortunately seldom come up in their gilded stories and songs with any real roses. It is particularly galling therefore that no credence can be given to the tale that the lovely *R. gallica versicolor*, known as Rosa Mundi, was named to commemorate the Fair Rosamund who died about 1176.

> Rosamund, the fayre daughter of Walter, Lord Clifford, concubine to King Henry II (poisoned by Queen Eleanor as some thought), died at Woodstocke, where King Henry had made for her a house of wonderful working so that no man or woman could come to her but that was instructed by the king: the house was named Labyrinthus ... wrought like unto a knot in a garden, called a maze; but it was commonly said that lastly the Queene came to her by a clue of thriddle or silk, and so dealt with her that she lived not long after; but when she was dead she was buried at Godstone in a house of nunnes, beside Oxford, with these verses on her tombe:
> *Hic jacet in tumba Rosa Mundi, non Rosa Munda*
> *Non redolet, sed olet, quae redolere solet*

Peter Coates quotes this account from the sixteenth-century chronicler and antiquary, John Stow, and translates Fair Rosamund's obituary as follows. It is not complimentary:

> Here rose the graced, not rose the chaste, reposes
> The scent that rises is no scent of roses.

It will be noted that Stow's version of the tale falls in with the medieval troubadour's imagery of the secret, marvelled palace of the lady (as well as with the Theseus/Minotaur legend of Knossos where some of the first known roses are frescoed on the walls: indeed it has

The following pages show plates 1–4

been suggested that the labyrinth represents a multifoliate rose bush with its twisting, barbed branches). Be that as it may, Rosamund's role as the king's mistress and her assassination are less romantic. But the Rosa Mundi rose is probably no older than Stow himself. Matthew de L'Obel (after whom the well-known blue annual lobelia is named) gave a description in 1581 which could be of this rose, yet there is no record of it in England – which is where, after all, it ought to be – until 100 years after L'Obel wrote. And then Thomas Fuller writes that 'the rose of roses had its first being in this city' – 'this city' being Norwich. A reference a couple of years earlier, in 1659, refers to it as a new rose which had occurred as a *gallica* sport in Norfolk.

We must take it, therefore, that the real flowering of the medieval rose was not in horticulture but in art. In this period symbolism and imagery entered into all parts of life so that the rose epitomizes perfection in painting and architecture (*Ut rosa flos florum sic est domus domorum*)[4] appears again and again in artefacts as small as illuminated capitals in books of hours and missals or as in the great Gothic cathedrals. In the latter the famous rose windows at Chartres and Laon in France and York and Lincoln (the 'Dean's Eye') in England are the culmination of those circular windows that had become more and more daring from the early middle ages since their introduction by Abbot Suger of St Denis. Their shape, so far from any botanical rose, reverts to the circularity (itself reflecting perfection) of one of the origins of the word 'rose' – *rota*, or wheel. At Chartres, for instance, the great west window has a central disc surrounded by twelve oval spokes while on the periphery small circular windows make a chaplet of roses in themselves. It is no doubt significant that Chartres was the first of the great churches to be dedicated to the Virgin: in France those at Paris, Amiens, Laon, Rouen and Rheims followed.

By fortunate chance or, it could be equally said, transparent inevitability, the great period of Mariolatry and rose symbolism coincides with a peak in European painting. There was the need to create religious works for proliferating churches, every altar of which required at least one triptych, and rich patrons to pay for them, who are often seen kneeling in the foreground. Here we see late medieval roses again and again.

One of the best known is Jan van Eyck's 'Virgin of the Fountain,' which was painted in 1439 and is now in the Koninklijk Museum, Antwerp. The Virgin, in a night-blue robe, stands on a floral and armorial tapestry, the back of which is held up behind her by two flying angels. Behind this is a raised flower bed, four bricks high, filled with red roses.

Some twenty years earlier The Master of the Little Paradise Garden (who worked in Germany at the turn of the fourteenth century) painted the enchanting picture which gives him his name. It is an altogether more primitive scene (in the painterly sense) and packed with symbolism. Inside a machicolated castle wall a childlike Virgin sits reading. Behind her a raised flower bed contains blue irises, the same colour as her gown, gilly flowers and other blossoms, while the turf at her feet is studded with madonna lilies, strawberries, cowslips, lilies of the valley and a fine single peony. There are birds too: a kingfisher, a yellow hammer and, symbolic of death and resurrection, a goldfinch. Various people, including the Christ-child playing a kind of horizontal harp, sit about. Water is being ladled from a well and here 'like a rose that is planted beside the waters' is a multi-petalled rose bush in full flower.

Further rose garden and symbolic rose paintings occur in private and public collections – though sadly perhaps less frequently at the altar for which they were painted – throughout the world.

One more description must suffice. Stephen Lochner's 'Madonna and Child in the Rose Arbour' (Wallraf-Richatz Museum, Cologne) was painted about 1450. The crowned Madonna (and there are jewelled roses in her crown) sits holding the Child. She is surrounded by child-angels who busily make music, playing portative organ, harp and lute. One is picking a flower from the delicate trellis which is entwined with semi-double red roses. All this produces the effect of the Virgin's being enshrined in a bower of roses. As it does so, it epitomizes for us, 500 years later, the atmosphere of that late flowering of chivalry, courtliness and, above all, of faith; a time in which the rose, that most perfect flower, although not a part, as today, of everyone's garden, was in truth a part of everyone's life.

[1] A.U Pope, *An Introduction to Persian Art Since the Seventeenth Century AD*

[2] Wilkins, pp105-106

[3] Such courtship, as Kenneth Clark points out, is so called 'because it was only in courts that one had time for those agreeable preliminaries'.

[4] 'As the rose is the flower of flowers so is this the house of all houses,' carved in the Chapter House of York Minster.

Chapter 3

The Wild Rose Tamed

It has already been seen that since earliest times wild roses have been taken into cultivation and grown for their virtues. Perhaps these were first of simple floral beauty and fragrance. Then, with increasing sophistication and technology, man discovered that some roses were fit for the production of rich oils and costly perfumes. Others he found had medicinal and culinary contributions to offer. The actual number of rose types concerned with these aspects, however, was and is remarkably small. As time went on, the range of roses appeared to increase, but it was mainly through the vegetative propagation of those bud sports (mutant forms) which had been observed to be significantly distinct from their parents.

Even with the flood of roses offered by nurseries from the beginning of the nineteenth century and exhaustive programmes of hybridization, the number of rose species involved remained, and still remains, very limited. Only about five per cent of the wild roses which are strewn about the world have been significantly used by rose breeders. What then of the other ninety-five per cent?

They interest us at several levels. Fundamentally their importance is as wild plants which, from common ancestors, have developed characteristics which make each a successful plant in the habitat in which it finds itself and to which it is perfectly adapted. Were each wild rose not a successful organism we would know nothing of it, for it would not have survived. No doubt there were many that are part of that history of the rose which can never be written. The 100 or 150 wild rose species which do exist are, with a very few exceptions, those which were on the earth when man came along, so short a time in evolutionary terms has been man's sojourn on the planet.

Shorter still, as has been seen, is the period in which he has affected roses in any significant way. Yet now, while finding it possible even to manipulate chromosomes and genes and hence manufacture new species, man is a much more serious threat to the continued existence of wild species. The progress of agriculture and forestry in all parts of the world takes little heed of plants which apparently lack economic value. Unfortunately, once lost, a species cannot be reconstituted: each has a unique genetic complement and none can be disregarded. The potential of the rose is in every species.

Predictably, early rosarians looked for the differences that occurred by chance in the roses they possessed. When the sexuality of plants became understood enough to make deliberate crosses possible, it was the extension of the colour range which was pre-eminent in man's mind. As we know, as with the introduction of the Austrian copper and Austrian yellow hybrids, such single-mindedness can introduce susceptibility to disease and reduction in scent. Later breeders, while not being oblivious to visual impact (and it must be remembered that the breeding of one good new rose is an enormously costly operation attended often by numerous failures, so the rose has to sell), have also been conscious of vigour, frost-hardiness in cold areas, disease resistance, good foliage and so on. No doubt there are species hitherto untapped still to be brought into the family tree of garden roses.

A plant species may be defined as an organism which breeds true from seed. Collect ripe hips from *R. eglanteria* in an English hedgerow, sow the seeds, and *R. eglanteria* will result. Do the same from the rose 'Peace' – if good seed can be found – and it is unlikely that a single plant will resemble the parent: the modern Hybrid Teas have such a rag-bag of genes that no certain prediction can be made as to what will result. This is of course why garden roses are propagated vegetatively. Species by comparison are constant. Yet they too change over evolutionary time as the tiny variations in new seedlings are better fitted to the equally gradual yet inexorable changes in environment and habitat.

Such changes help to explain the fact that there are *wild* roses of all colours from white through pink to scarlet and purple (presumably different insects of varying tastes are expected to pollinate them) and that *R. spinosissima* is twenty-five inches tall while *R. gigantea* can have growths twenty-five feet long: obviously different attributes are needed for success if Scottish sea-shores or Burmese jungles are to be colonized equally successfully by this same genus *Rosa*. Realization of such aspects of different yet parallel development can tell us a lot about the roses we grow. It will be seen that those with hooked spines are likely to be climbers or have climbing species in their parentage – though no rose actually *climbs*, there are no tendrils, or suckers or twining ability, it only scrambles; up go those long lax shoots into another bush or tree and the downward-pointing prickles prevent it falling. True shrubs have straight prickles for defence purposes only. A mixture of prickle-types in a garden rose will indicate a mixture of parentage. Extraordinarily, the Chinese *R. marrettii* has upward-facing prickles. Whatever the reason for it this variation cannot be entirely fortuitous.

It might be thought odd, or at least unnecessary, that species diversification should exist over small areas (there are over a dozen roses in Britain alone), but we have to note habitat variation, which is highly significant to plants; those most successful in each type of habitat or micro-habitat survive to reproduce and develop what we recognize as specific differences. There are roses which accept higher or lower soil lime content; some take shade while others insist on full sun; yet others depend upon perfect drainage at the root while the American *R. palustris* is rightly called, in both Latin and English, the marsh rose. Hence it colonizes a site otherwise unused by its relations and lack of competition is an aid to individual success. Each species therefore inhabits that area whose conditions suit it best. Yet, obviously, habitats and hence species overlap and in such conditions natural hybrids do occur with recognizable characteristics of both parent species. Only if the resultant bi-specific plant is more efficient than either of its parents is it likely to colonize and set up in competition. However, it is the existence of such natural hybrids and the inevitable shadowy area between really distinct species which accounts for the differing number of species stated by different authorities.

It can be appreciated then that this genus *Rosa* inhabits much of the landmass of the northern hemisphere. Some species have an enormous range – that of the Burnet Rose from Iceland to China is described on page 157 – while others have a very restricted range: *R. montezumae*, for instance inhabits only a relatively small area of New Mexico. In many cases species overlap, even with several of their relatives.

As discussed in the Appendix, not all rose species, even if they are geographically adjacent, can naturally interbreed. Such incompatibility helps to maintain specific constancy. On the other hand, species separated by oceans or mountain ranges often meet socially by man's agency in gardens and there crosses occur. To such acts of chance many of the ancestral (bi-specific) species and groups are attributed. Thus this collection of species provides what can be seen as a great gene bank of rose potential for our gardens' use.

John Goare's Cinnamon Roses

Rose species are also recognized, not merely as hybrid-fodder, but also as finished individuals worth bringing into gardens for their own sakes. It is worth looking, therefore, as some of the hundred or so species that are actually in cultivation. As the emphasis of this chapter is upon the natural rose, that is perhaps best done geographically. Three main areas deserve our attention in which all the forms of rose, from small bushes to tall scramblers, exist, developing their differences in parallel.

Western China and the Himalayan foothills can be taken as the epicentre of rose distribution, so today towards eighty-five per cent of species are found in the temperate Far East; before, to use the words from the 'Old Hundreth' hymn, 'Earth received her frame,' precursors of existing species moved westward into Europe and, while a land-bridge still existed, eastward into what is now North America. These two areas contain respectively around ten per cent and five per cent of wild roses.

The concern of this chapter is to review those roses which are wild species but which are either in cultivation or, in one or two cases, are no longer worthy of it. Species which, like *R. chinensis* or *R. wichuraiana,* have much affected garden hybrids are described elsewhere and are of only passing interest here. In the Appendix the role of the ten sections of roses is considered in relation to the contribution that each has made to garden roses. It will be noted that while the *Cinnamomeae* had the most species of any (forty-eight), only two, the type species *R. cinnamomea* itself and *R. rugosa,* have been used at all much by rose breeders. Even these must be seen as minor strands: other members of the group that have taken or are taking part in hybridization programmes have done so relatively recently and will be referred to again.

But many close relations of the Cinnamon Rose are grown for their own natural beauty. The type species of the group is one such and, having a very wide geographical distribution, from western Europe (but not Britain) eastward to Japan, was in cultivation from early times, as Gerard (*Herball*, 1597) reports and illustrates:

> The Canel or Cinnamon Rose, or the rose smelling like Cinnamon, hath shoots of a brown colour, four cubits high, beset with thorny prickles, and leaves like unto those of Eglantine, but smaller and Greene, of the savour or smell of Cinnamon. Whereof it took its name, and not of the smell of his flowers (as some have deemed) which have little or no savour at all.

Gerard goes on to mention both a double and a single form. In fact, and in spite of the name, the cinnamon scent is hardly at all noticeable (could this scent, like that of musk, have been lost since the time of Gerard and Parkinson?). As a diagnostic aid, the huge leafy stipules, perhaps the biggest in the whole genus, are far more reliable. Gerard's measure of a cubit is the distance from the tip of the middle finger to the elbow, about thirty inches, and a height of seven feet is usual – both then and now.

From nearly the central point of the Cinnamon Rose's range comes a fine batch of wild *Cinnamomeae*. One of the best was named after French missionary-collector, Père David, who first discovered it. *R. davidii* was brought into cultivation through the collections of E. H. Wilson in 1908. He described it as growing in thickets and attaining around five feet in height. If it likes its site in the garden, it exceeds this and proves to be a most worthwhile plant.

Related and growing in similar areas in western China (Moupine and western Szechuan) at toward 12,000 feet are, among others, *Rr. caudata, corymbulosa* and *prattii*. Miss Ellen Willmott thought highly of the former and it flowered for the first time in Britain in her garden at Warley Place, Essex, in 1911. As so many of the early twentieth-century rose collections were grown at Warley, it is fitting that one of these plants should commemorate the owner, one of the greatest rose enthusiasts of all time. *R. willmottiae* is a tall yet very delicate mauve-pink species which E. H. Wilson found on the Tibetan frontier of western China. It first flowered in Veitch's renowned Coombe Wood nursery in England in 1907.

Without detailed botanical descriptions, these closely related pink-flowered *Cinnamomeae* roses are apt to sound so alike as not to deserve full specific rank. Suffice it to say here that in spite of close geographical proximity, adaptation to different habitats has indeed produced clearly discernible differences which, moreover, breed true as true species must.

Another group including *R. bella* and *R. holodonta* is centred round the glorious *R. moyesii*, introduced from north-west China. Again the introduction to gardens was through E. H. Wilson and Messrs Veitch in the first decade of this century. Although he was not the first person to discover it, Wilson must have been instrumental in the choice of name: the Reverend J Moyes belonged to the China Inland Mission and was of great help to Wilson in his travels in that area.

Rosa moyesii makes a great fountain of a bush, up to fifteen feet high, with relatively small foliage and clear blood-red flowers. These are followed by magnificent cascades of vermilion-red fruit, bottle shaped and an inch and a half in length. This striking plant is perhaps the best known of all Himalayan rose species and several selections have been made of what may be distinctive forms, both in the wild and in cultivation. 'Geranium' is one raised at the Royal Horticultural Society Gardens at Wisley, Surrey, in England: dwarfer in habit, it is, if anything, even more spectacular in flower and fruit than its parent. *R.* x *highdownenis* is a seedling of *R. moyesii* which was produced in 1928 at Sir Frederick Stern's famous chalk-pit garden in Sussex. Here the flowers are deep pink but the fruit is still vivid scarlet-orange and produced in formidable profusion.

At the other end of the size scale is the remarkable little *R. farreri persetosa.* Hips of this rose had been collected by Reginald Farrer in southern Kansu province (north-west China) in 1915 and one of the seedlings was germinated in E. A. Bowles's garden. It turned into this highly distinctive rose. The branches are entirely covered with bristly spines where, to quote Bowles's description:

> Before the flower buds open the whole bush seems set with coral beads. The open flowers are of a peculiarly soft warm pink, which the light golden anthers cause to glow in the same way as in the larger flowers of that beautiful old Briar, *Rosa andersonii*. The leaves are so small and delicate in outline that the bush has a dainty finished look peculiarly its own, not only when the grey-green of young leaves sets off the salmon-pink flowers, but again, when touches of purple and crimson appear in autumn along with the brilliant coral-red of the tiny hips.

A gratified raiser may be forgiven a certain partiality but any observant grower of this lovely plant will happily accept the description.

Asiatic in origin, too, is the Scots Burnet Rose which extends throughout Europe and Asia. Yellow variants occurred early among those nineteenth-century selections begun near Perth. There are also fine yellow subspecies such as the Siberian *R. spinosissima hispida;* this plant was, confusingly, known at one stage as the 'American Yellow Rose'. Other, especially Asiatic, members of its class *Pimpinellifoliae,* exhibit that colour even more clearly: *R. foetida*, of course, through the Pernet Roses, brought yellow into our modern garden roses. But our concern here is with wild species.

Because of its name, it seems right to begin with *R. primula*, introduced from Turkistan in 1911. Its primrose yellow flowers are borne in late May, in the midst of delicate incense-scented foliage, on a strong thorny bush six feet or so high. This rose was confused for some time with a compatriot, yet actually very distinct plant, *R. ecae.*

Dr J. E. T. Aitchison introduced several good plants, and indeed other roses, but must have felt particularly drawn to this little rose as he used his wife's initials to coin its name. Sourer commentators might consider his action, in view of this rose's extreme prickliness, a back-handed compliment. *R. ecae* has shining flowers among ferny foliage, like golden sovereigns seen through rippled water. Though recorded in its native habitat as forming hedges with gooseberry and buckthorn, in northern Europe it needs a warm and sheltered corner.

From farther East, following the Burnet trail, come more yellow *Pimpinellifoliae*. *R. xanthina* has been grown in the West only since 1907, but it seems likely, in view of its semi-double clear yellow flowers, that it was one of the many plants already existing in garden forms which have been brought from China over the last 300 years. A single type known as *R. xanthina spontanea* came later and appears to be the wild original. The frequently offered 'Canary Bird' is a good selected form with deep golden yellow flowers on a six-foot bush.

R. hugonis is not dissimilar but is paler in flower – paler even than *R. primula* – and has more noticeably bristly shoots. It was first collected by the Reverend Hugh Scallan, whose name it bears. Even after its short May flower display is over, the fernlike foliage is sufficiently ornamental to earn it its place.

All these Burnet rose relations differ markedly from the type, not merely in their generally much greater size but in their red, rather than black, fruits. They interbreed readily in captivity and have given several fine hybrids which maintain the early yellow-flowering habit, but usually on a larger or more extended scale. *R.* x *cantabrigiensis (hugonis* x *sericea*) was an early success with fine two-inch wide flowers.

The last-named species belongs to a small group of oriental roses whose immediately obvious difference is that they are, almost invariably, four-petalled. (It will be remembered that there is a six-petalled plant: the Minoan rose depicted at Knossos.) Having simple leaves it can be referred to as *Rosa* or *Hulthemia, persica* although it does in fact normally bear five-petalled flowers. These are the roses which differ from the archetypal pentamerous pattern upon which so much legend and myth is based; but only this little *sericeae* group really possesses the difference.

A reduction of floral parts is not often a recommendation to grow a plant, but one of the group, *R. omeiensis pteracantha*, has a virtue unique in its genus. The floral display is good – masses of white dog-rose flowers in May – but not outstanding. When young, however, the great strong shoots (which rocket from nine to thirteen feet high) are a deep red, a colour shared by the wide-based prickles. Each base meets the next and, seen against the light, the whole shoot seems bathed in a sunrise glow.

This plant was discovered in Yunnan by another French missionary priest, the Abbé Delavay who sent seed to M. de Vilmorin. Its remarkable habit was thus first seen in Europe at Les Barres at the turn of the century.

The discussion of Asiatic roses has so far remained with those species which are naturally of bush habit though varying from one to three to fifteen feet in height. The *synstylae* group of twenty-three species should now be considered. All are more or less of robust scrambling habit, including the biggest rose of all, the vast *R. leschenaultiana* from South India. As the latter is probably not in cultivation and also is very frost tender (and clearly it is not easy to protect a plant that reaches sixty-five feet in height) it need detain us no more here. Nor need the important members *Rr. multiflora, wichuraiana, moschata* and others which have been so much a part of hybridization programmes and which are described elsewhere in this book. But there are plenty of others.

Just as *R. primula* can be seen to eptiomize yellow-flowered rose species, so perhaps, should *R. rubus* be the focal point of this section, the name being more common as the generic one for the brambles, the habit of which is not dissimilar, with their sprays of generally creamy white flowers. All but a couple are vigorous ramblers.

R. rubus is one such fine strong plant for billowing through a hedgerow. The scented, rich cream flowers are the earliest to open of its group and each has a distinctive central boss of orange stamens. It will reach twelve feet in height or spread. Rather similar but smaller is the closely related *R. helenae* which has the virtue of brilliant hips. Both were introduced from central China in 1907.

R. longicuspis also came from China at about the same time, although the exact date is unknown. The flowers are carried in enormous clusters, between one and two hundred in each; with the annual shoot growth approaching twenty feet in length, the plant can be a remarkable sight, while the scent is distinctively that of ripe bananas.

The handsome *R. sinowilsonii* has been suggested as being synonymous with the last-named but Graham Thomas has no doubt of the difference. Certainly it does not share the frost-hardiness of *R. longicuspis*, having been found by E. H. Wilson in Szechuan in 1904 at altitudes of only around 3,200 feet above sea level. 'No rose,' says Mr Thomas, 'is so handsome in leaf, and it would be worth a place on any warm sunny wall for that character alone.' The seven long corrugated leaflets are dark shining green above with plum-purple reverses. It is apt that such a rose should commemorate 'Chinese Wilson,' as he was affectionately known, who enriched our gardens with so many good plants.

R. brunonii (a rather inelegant latinization of Brown – Robert Brown is the dedicatee) is the plant which masqueraded for some time as the Old Musk Rose (see page 84). Often now referred to as the Himalayan Musk Rose, this is a very vigorous scrambler with viciously hooked prickles. A single plant needs plenty of space; the well-known specimen at Kiftsgate Court in Gloucestershire, England, was over thirty-three feet high and more than that across. This, in fact, was of the rather hardier form which originated at the famous garden called La Mortola in Italy and which is available under that name. The heavily fragrant white flowers open in June and July.

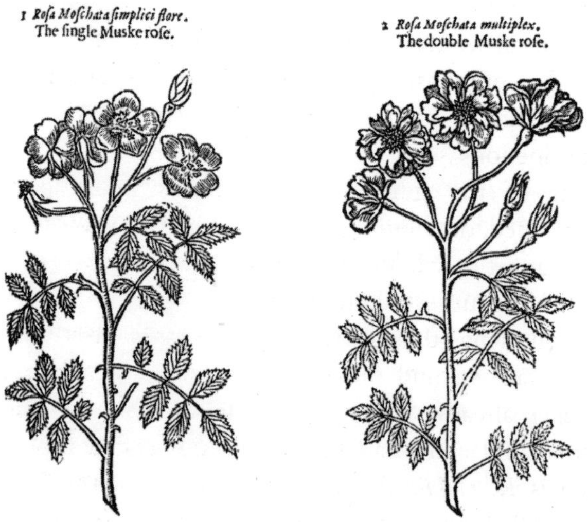

Known to the Elizabethans, as Gerard's illustrations show, the true musk rose was subsequently lost to cultivation until the 1950s

The same Gloucestershire garden is also renowned as being the source of the remarkable form of *R. filipes* which bears its name 'Kiftsgate'. This is no doubt the biggest hardy rose in cultivation: old plants are fifty feet or more across and forty feet high. Where space allows, nothing could be finer with its pale green leaves, bronze-tinted when young, and its great late-June cascades of scented white flowers. (It has, unfortunately, also been frequently planted through careless over-recommendation at the base of declining apple trees in small suburban gardens where it has been seen as the ultimate in ground cover plants.) The original species is yet another Wilson plant from western China, introduced in 1908.

The emphasis given to Asiatic roses and the outstandingly productive years of the E. H. Wilson introductions serve to underline that area as a central point of the genus. By no means have all been mentioned, only enough of the distinctive types to serve as an appetite-whetter for further reading and, it is to be hoped, for successful cultivations.

Following the distribution of roses westward, in Turkestan we find those yellow species *R. ecae* and *R. primula*, already described, and meet others which are rather similar in Asia Minor and south-east Europe. One such is *R. rapinii*, the wild single form of the Sulphur Rose (*R. hemisphaerica*) which was for so long the only double yellow rose known to man. The species, beautiful thought it is, is no easier to cultivate than its derivative.

From this area, too, comes the famed *R. persica*. Very atypical and difficult to grow, only in recent years has it been possible to make any real use of its undoubted potential for hybridization. This will be discussed in more detail later. On first sight that little suckering bush with its simple exstipulate greyish leaves resembles a prickly cistus or *Halimium*. The five-petalled yellow flowers, with a central scarlet zone, are similarly short lived. (Alfred Parson's charming portrait of it in the *Genus Rosa* shows two red-blotched petals in the very act of falling from a finished flower.) The first recorded mention of this plant is by Jussieu in his *Genera Plantarum* of 1789 and the introduction of living material to both France and England occurred the following year.

So different are its attributes from the rest of *Genus Rosa* that is now generally agreed to give this plant full generic status. Dumortier's name (1824), as the first published, is used. *Hulthemia persica*, then, is clearly of some considerable interest: as a very primitive rose it seems to have been left behind by its more evolutionary adaptive relations. Man, it seems, is now helping it to catch up.

While of the twenty-three *synstylae* roses most are Asiatic, the section does have European representatives. Of these the Mediterranean *R. sempervirens* and the more generally distributed *R. arvensis* are those which have contributed thin strands to garden-rose development.

Europe also has members of the huge *Cinnamomeae* group, though they are not much grown. *R. pendulina* is a lovely plant with purplish almost thornless stems and dark-pink flowers. Both Gerard and Parkinson refer to a rose without thorns – it will be remembered that the symbolism of such a plant was considerable – but there can be no certainty that it was this. As Miss Wilmott says:

> The Alpine Rose[1] is one of the great ornaments of all the mountains of central and southern Europe, for both flowers and fruit are beautiful. It ranges from the Alps westward to the Pyrenees and eastward to Greece.

It is, of course, a parent of the Boursalt Roses but in its own right or in its double form 'Moriettii' should not be so neglected in gardens.

Other significant European roses belong to the *Caninae* section. Only the eglantine has been used in hybridization to any extent and unfortunately to the point at which, though florally bigger and brighter (and susceptible to powdery mildew and even blackspot), it has lost much of its famous foliar fragrance. It might be better to look at its south-east European relation (in fact the species overlap geographically), *R. glutinosa.* The dwarf Dalmatian form, with pink flowers and deep red fruits, is only eighteen inches high and has, perhaps, the most aromatic foliage of all wild roses. *R. serafinii* is closely related.

Further leaf fragrance comes from the wide-ranging *R. villosa (pomifera),* the Apple Rose. The leaves are grey-green and noticeably downy; while the clear pink flowers are attractive it is the big round crimson fruits which in autumn make the main display. A fine semi-double form with mahogany-coloured 'apples' is known as Wolley-Dod's Rose, having been raised in the garden of the reverend gentleman of that name.

There is little doubt that with current interest in plant associations both in the garden and as cut-flower arrangements in the home, *R. rubrifolia* is the most grown European rose species. In the wild it extends on the uplands from the Pyrenees to southern Austria and different collections vary in the strength of the colour of the leaves. It is for these that the plant is particularly grown, the colour shading from grey-purple when in a sunny position to a mauve-tinged green when grown in shade. Both flowers and fruit are complementary.

Moving across the Atlantic in this short geographical survey of wild roses, the Cinnamon Rose section again becomes important, and it will be noted that the basic habit of roses native in the New World is a free-standing bushes and not climbers (the Cherokee Rose, it will be remembered, is an Asiatic that has taken out naturalization papers).

Rosa blanda is the American equivalent of the Alpine Rose. It extends right across the continent in damp, rocky sites from Labrador to Vancouver Island and has predictably unarmed often reddish stems which carry the clusters of pink flowers. Like *R. pendulina* this rose, especially the eastern forms, is extremely frost-tolerant.

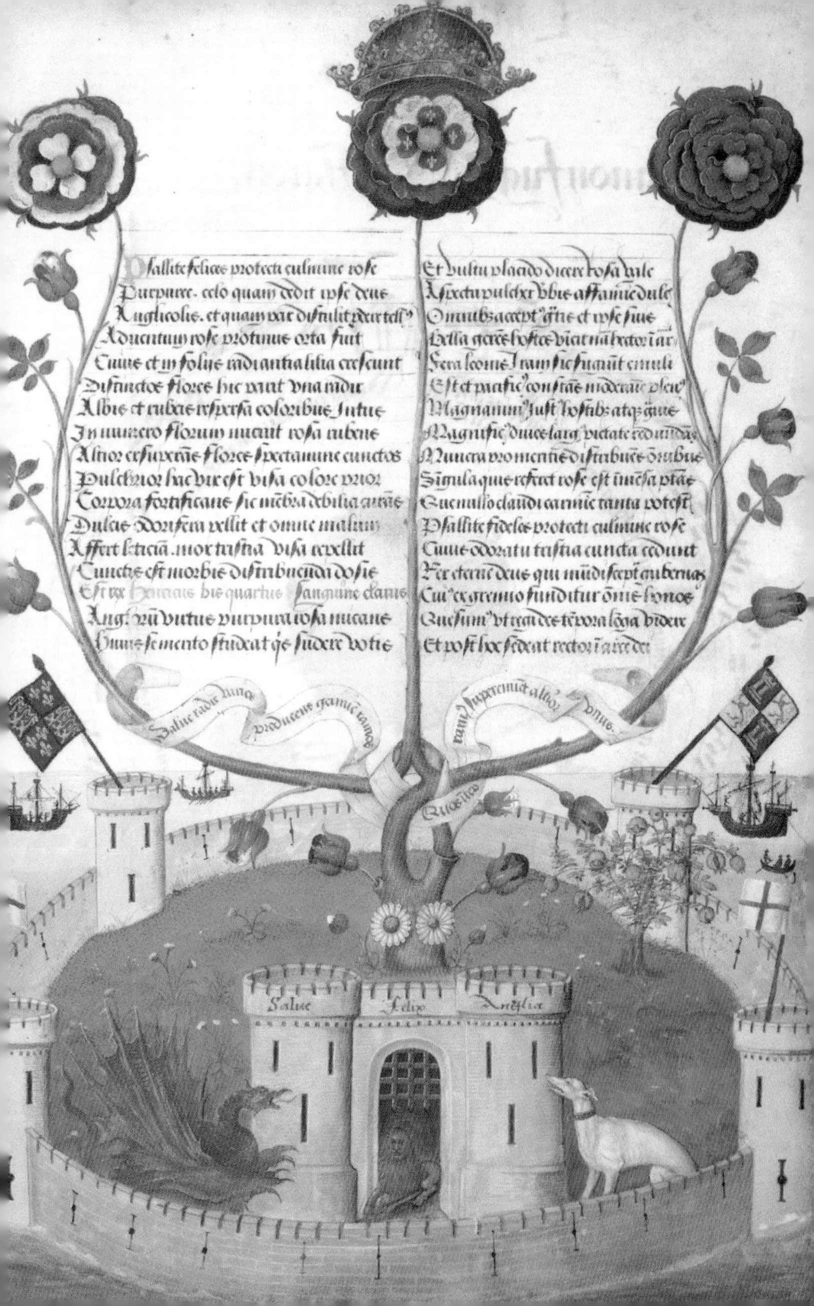
Salue
Felix
Anglia

dieu
et
mon
droit

Such a virtue has been the reason for several North American roses, such as *R. acicularis*, to be used in the search for frost-hardy hybrids.

Other *Cinnamomeae* here include the Cluster Rose, *R. pisocarpa*, a slender western coastal species; this makes a dense bush with lilac-pink heads of flower. It has been regarded by some as little more than a geographical form of *R. californica* with which it shares the eastern part of its range. The latter, however, is a much bigger plant, reaching ten feet or so in height, and the hips are pleasantly edible after they have been exposed to frost. In cultivation the beautiful semi-double form, known slightly exaggeratedly as 'Plena,' is more commonly seen. This most attractive plant has ferny foliage and big heads of dark pink flowers which fade to rose and near-purple.

R. woodsii from central and western North America has been superseded in gardens by a particularly good form known as *R. w. fendleri*. Here a strong five-foot bush carries bright lilac-pink flowers and showers of sealing-wax red hips long into winter after the leaves have fallen. The bigger *R. nutkana* has similar virtues.

A further group of North American roses is gathered around *R. carolina* (which in spite of its name is the state flower of Iowa) and includes *R. nitida, R. foliolosa* and *R. virginiana*. They rather take the place there of the Scots Briers with their low suckering growth building up to thickets of bristly stems and happy acceptance (especially with the last named) of poor sandy soils. What they also have, like so many East Coast shrubs, is spectacular autumn colour. For this reason especially, Miss Willmott commends *R. nitida* as the most beautiful of eastern North American roses.

Two or three roses get as far south as New Mexico and this must be seen as a dwindling away as conditions cease to be acceptable even to highly adaptive roses. One is a *canina* relative, *R. montezumae*, not in cultivation. More interesting is the Sacramento Rose (*R. stellata mirifica*) which comes from the uplands of New Mexico and southern Texas. It makes a low shrub developing into dense thickets. The prickles are distinctively ivory-coloured and the flowers are a deep rose-purple. In cultivation this rare species is obviously a plant only for the specialist rosarian with a hot corner available; but it indicates, as perhaps do some of the western Asiatic species of not dissimilar habitat, that will to adapt to a very atypically rosaceaous environment. It also underlines the great variation that the genus exhibits from such dwarf shrubs of semi-desert to great scramblers of subtropical rain forest. We should not be surprised, therefore, nor cease to be amazed at what we as gardeners are offered.

[1] Not to be confused with the 'Alpenrose' which is *Rhododendron ferrugineum* and no relation, although Rhodos/dendron does translate as 'rose tree'.

Chapter 4

Renaissance and Romantic Roses: 1500–1800

By 1500 the arts of the Renaissance were at their peak; only a decline, some would suggest, into the coarseness of Mannerism was ahead. They lighten again as we move into the eighteenth century, as grandiloquent baroque is succeeded by delicate rococo.

Throughout these periods, however, the basis is still classicism in one form or another. It is most easily recognized in Palladio's churches in Venice or his villas in the Veneto of the sixteenth century and in the pedimented and pilastered façades of British and American domestic buildings even after 1800.

The relative stability of these 300 years, though not without periods of internecine strife and interstate conflict, made it possible for the art of garden making to be reborn. The grandest gardens were associated, of course, with the grandest houses and the palaces of rich potentates, lay and religious. Bramante's garden for the Belvedere (planned in 1503), for example, linked two parts of the Vatican garden for Pope Julius II in a spectacularly architectural fashion.

We see those rich city-states of Italy as places in which gardening began to show itself outside of those cloistered religious houses which had kept a shoot of classical horticulture alive.

Within the great gardens, with their ramps, flights of steps, statues and alcoves, and complicated topiary – none of which offered places for roses – there was very often that garden within a garden, the *giardino segreto.* Here grew flowers, for medicine, for herbal use and for simple floral beauty. Here grew roses.

In Italy too were set up the first botanic gardens, as we know them, in the western world. Pisa and Padua began theirs (to support schools of medicine at a time when most medicine was plant-based) in the 1540s. In essence, behind their high walls they too were *giardini segreti.* With medicine and subsequently the science of botany dictating the increasing range of plants grown, they grew those roses known to be medically useful, especially of course the Apothecary's Rose, *R. gallica officinalis*, and species new to western science, *R. moschata* and *R. cinnamomea.*

We see the early part of this period first as one of consolidation as those roses locally wild and those which had apparently been in cultivation from time immemorial were gathered together. And gathered together in gardens with an observant staff in which bud sports would most likely be noticed and propagated, and where chance seedlings might be recognized to have some significance (one may forget that over 200 years were to pass before the sexuality of plants was understood and intentional crosses were made).

Other factors are important. By 1500 printing was becoming instrumental in the dissemination of ideas and techniques. Not long before this date there were only incredibly beautiful but utterly laboursome manuscript texts, rather like horticultural bestiaries. Illustrations in the form of simple woodcuts soon began to add interest to the printed word (usually difficult to read in black letter gothic), but it was not until the magnificent folio *De Historia Stirpium* by Leonard Fuchs came out in 1542, its plates drawn and hand-coloured from life (the back page shows the artist Albrecht Meyer actually engaged in drawing a plant) that we can confidently relate picture to plant. It never ceases to amaze, also, that many of Fuchs's names are simple Linnaean-like binomials which, adopted by the latter, are still valid today, more than four centuries later.

The time, then, seemed right for a gentle explosion of all arts, gardening not excepted; there was relative peace, and there was enormous wealth in the hands of patrons, some of them of taste and with the ability to disseminate information in a way never before possible. There was a fourth concomitant: it began to be an age of colonial expansion. At first that did not merely mean military conquest; it meant exploration (often little more than a newly discovered coastal strip), chart-making and the collection of plants and animals of possible economic or merely curiosity value to bring home and prove the trip had actually taken place.

Those voyages which followed Columbus's first visit to the New World in 1492 are typical. One, around 1530, brought back potatoes – no doubt of greater benefit to Europeans than all the Eldorado gold of the Conquistadors. The circumnavigation of Africa in search of an eastward sea route to the Indies soon followed, and opened an alternative to the old, land spice-route, along which plants had always come to adorn a rich man's garden.

It would be useful then, before examining this flurry of activity, to reassess those roses in cultivation in Europe at this time.

For many people, it was only the wild briers which were available, all more or less of dog-rose type and ranging geographically from the Mediterranean *R. sempervirens* to *R. canina* itself in north Britain. Doubtless particularly attractive forms were brought into a castle demesne or thrust into a quick-set hedge in a yeoman-farmer's garden, but they add little to the development of a body of cultivated roses. That their simple beauty was recognized by civilization which was now beginning to be able to appreciate the countryside aesthetically, rather than seeing it only as the haunt of voracious beasts and even more dangerous men, is clear. To understand this we have only to look a little later at Nicholas Hilliard's famous and exquisite miniature of a somewhat 'greenery-yallery' Elizabethan gallant leaning against an oak and with a blush dog-rose flowering between him and the painter.

The sweetbriers too were widely cultivated. Although known for many years, due to a Linnaean confusion, as *R. rubiginosa*, it is now back to the eglantine of the poets: botanically *R. eglanteria*. The name derives from the Latin *aculeatus*, meaning prickly, and John Parkinson's seventeenth-century description supports this, it being 'armed with the cruellest sharpe and strong thrones and quicker set, than is any other rose either wilde or tame'. Sweetbrier was then, as now, the ideal garden hedge – impenetrable, elegant in flower and fruit with a fragrance from the leaves, especially after a shower of rain, that is completely delightful. Variants in flower colour and number of petals have from time to time turned up; Parkinson described a double form in 1629 and Alfred Parsons' charming plate used to illustrate this species in *The Genus Rosa* in fact the semi-double 'Janet's Pride' found wild in a Cheshire hedgerow. It was this plant which prompted Lord Penzance to begin the selection and hybridization which produced the nineteenth-century Penzance Briers.

Very soon, however, after 1500, we find definite references, not just charming hearsay or legend, to other roses of great significance. The records come not from travellers such as Hakluyt or general historians such as Stow, but from writers to whom plants and plant lore were a major concern. These were herbalist–botanists changing to botanist–herbalists, as the emphasis, with the accumulation of more and better information, developed from alchemy to medicine. It is not easy to accept from a viewpoint of even only a couple of centuries or so ahead (so short a time in the development of the rose or indeed any other plant) that Turner, Gerard, Parkinson or Blackwell were still basing some of their thoughts, practices and writings upon Paracelsian ideas.

Paracelsus (1493–1541) extended the idea of the doctrine of signatures, which stated that a beneficent deity, having created man in His own image, had also created plants to cure man's ills. All that had to be done was to put the right plant to the right disease – easier said than done of course – but that same deity provided clues in the resemblance of each useful plant, or part of it, to the organ of the body concerned. Remnants of the theory remain in the botanical names of many plants: pulmonaria (lungwort), hepatica (for the kidneys) and so on.

In parallel with the doctrine of signatures was the then generally accepted belief that human matter was composed of the four elements – earth, fire, air and water – and that an associated humour went with each: phlegmatic, choleric, sanguine and melancholic. Diagnosis of a patient's problems had to take these things

The following pages show plates 5–8

into careful consideration and, at a time when few effective medicines were not plant-based (leaving out 'eye of newt and tongue of frog' concoctions), the rose and its products were of prime importance. This will be examined in 'The Rose Consumed,' (page 192); suffice it to say here that most early treatises, our main source of information, have strong medicinal overtones. The rose with its actual curative properties, its delicious perfume capable of masking less agreeable smells and its mystique of perfection made it the ideal drug plant. That value is not yet fully superseded even to this day.

Most important is the only European reddish rose – *R. gallica.* This, it will be recalled, is the Rose of Provins, having among its form the brilliant Apothecary's Rose. Its ability to retain its scent when dried ensures that it will always be grown.

Rosa gallica is the first of what are now regarded and referred to as the prime 'five ancestors' of garden roses. Few important garden roses do not contain the blood of at least one and many contain that of several in consort. Although not nearly that colour itself, the deep velvety purplish-red of modern hybrid Teas usually indicates gallica blood several generations back.

In the earlier chapter, 'The Roses of the Ancients' it is shown to have been cultivated even in pre-classical times and was possibly the sacred rose of religious cults practiced by the Medes and Persians. It is likely to have been the Rose of Miletus of the Romans. Shepherd suggests that it was this rose which William Rufus pretended to want to see when he visited the nunnery of Romsey in Hampshire, England, at the end of the eleventh century (actually it was to try and get a glimpse of the beautiful Matilda, who subsequently married his brother Henry I).

The role of these roses in heraldry and religious symbolism has already been discussed (see 'Rosa Mundi: The Medieval Rose'). As the sixteenth and seventeenth centuries progressed the range of forms proliferated until, by the beginning of the nineteenth century, it is said that over 1,000 different cultivars existed. The Empress Josephine, for example, had towards 200 in her famous garden at Malmaison.

The basic red rose is the one with semi-double flowers and yellow stamens which appears in so many early fifteenth-century religious paintings, returning again and again as that century progressed, not least in the work of one of the century's greatest ornaments – Botticelli. There are baskets of red and white roses around the Virgin and Child enthroned between St John the Baptist and St John the Evangelist in the Bardi Altarpiece he painted for the chapel of Santo Spirito, Florence, in 1484. An enscrolled inscription around the roses reads '*Quasi plantazio rose in Jericho*' ('like those grown in Jericho'). In 'The Birth of Venus,' Botticelli's cool, yet erotic, ideal woman (the same woman whether she be the Virgin Mary or Venus, Goddess of Love) is borne ashore on her scallop-shell surfboard amid a cloud of blush and white roses.

The white roses in that painting seem to be *R. alba*, another of the five ancestors, with its softly grey-green foliage and long leafy sepals. While that too was reputedly grown by the Romans it is necessary to move into the post-1500 period to be sure that this is what is being referred to. It may, too, have been the Yorkist rose, though there is no particular reason why that inflammatory badge should not have been any of several white-petalled natives.

But with the 'Father of English Botany,' William Turner (predating Gerard's more famous *Herball* by nearly fifty years), we are on surer ground. Not only does the species get a description in Turner's book, but so too do certain cultivars: 'Maiden's Blush,' or in the French version 'Cuisse de Nymphe' – both very suitable descriptions for its delicate apple-blossom colouring. Slightly deeper is 'Cuisse de Nymphe Émue'. This is Miller's *R. incarnata* and Turner's 'Incarnacion Rose,' whose name means flesh-coloured. We may have legitimate doubts about the Yorkist legend, but there is little doubt its being the Jacobite emblem. As Alice Coats remarked: 'Long after the last echoes of the "Fifteen" and the "Forty-five" had died away, devoted adherents of the lost Jacobite cause still wore a white rose on the birthday of the Old Pretender, 10th June.' We see it engraved on surviving Jacobite drinking glasses for toasting 'the King over the Water' – again, the rose is being used as a symbol of secrecy (see page 19).

Not surprisingly with such an ancient and highly regarded rose, there are further named forms which date back to the sixteenth century or even earlier. As always we cannot with certainty go further than the first reputable written record, but clearly *semi-plena*, which makes an enormous ten-foot bush (like, says Shepherd, a great mock orange when in bloom) is safe enough in Turner's hands. *R. alba suaveolens* is the highly scented form once grown commercially in Bulgaria for the production of attar of roses, where, records Graham Thomas, it often surrounds the plantations of Damask roses.

The presumption that *R. alba* is a true species is of long standing, especially as it has been found growing apparently wild in many places, including Britain. Shepherd suggests that it might be a natural hybrid between *R. gallica* and *R. corymbifera*, yet the dominance of the former's red pigmentation seems to militate against it, for Albas are always pale. More recently, and with the benefit of modern cytological techniques, a Damask–dog-rose cross has been preferred.

The soft green, semi-double *R. damascena* is itself also a hybrid or, to more exact, a compendium of hybrids both of which have their own derivatives. *R. gallica* is believed to be common to both. These possible interspecific Damasks appear under several names and confusion is not always easy to avoid. *R. gallica* x *R. phoenicea* (an otherwise undistinguished species, though it will be remembered as perhaps being one half of the holy rose – *R. richardii*) is supposed to be the Summer Damask. Likewise *R. gallica* x *R. moschata* may be the Autumn Damask, Monthly Damask, Quatre Saisons, Rose of Paestum and Pompeian rose. Botanically it is now called *R.* x *bifera*, a name recalled from Pliny who referred to its biannual flowering.

Uses in classical times have already been mentioned and clearly the authentic fame of *R.* x *bifera* persisted into the Moorish Empire. It is known to have been cultivated as a source of attar of roses in Syria as early as the tenth century. But close in many ways as was the early Renaissance to Islam, the earliest western European references are surprisingly late. The traveller Hakluyt states that the Damask rose was brought to England 'by Doctor Linaker, King Henry the Seventh and King Henry the Eighth's Physician'. Linacre died in 1521, but the report gains some corroboration from the famous botanist Matthiolus' saying in 1544 that a Monthly rose had been in Italy for only a few years. Dr Monardes, writer of a Spanish text (1551) on the roses of Persia and Alexandria, also remarks that it had only been available in Europe for thirty years. He says too that it was so named because it came from Damascus, which disposes of another romantic Crusader story.

Why such a desirable plant disappeared from the western European scene for so long can only be pointless supposition, but one theory is of interest: that its particular and desirable attribute of remontancy is so much less apparent in cooler climes that it could have been about without anyone noticing.

Be that as it may, once it was brought (or brought back) into cultivation, it quickly became a favourite and any distinctive bud sports were cherished. The famous pink and white York and Lancaster Damask appeared at about this time but, sadly, little credence can be given to the legend that it appeared as if by a miracle in a Wiltshire monastery, in the year 1485 when that dynastic Lancaster and York marriage between Henry VII and Elizabeth of York took place. However, other named Damasks can more definitely be dated – as, for example 'Celsiana', a fine pure semi-double which was known before 1750.

The next of the five ancestors is the Musk rose, *R. moschata*. This too has provided much cause for confusion, not least because its name is so similar to *R. muscosa* (now *R. centifolia muscosa*), the Moss rose. Another area of confusion is that plants going erroneously under that name were, until quite recently, its only manifestation. Graham Thomas explains the situation in a chapter entitled 'The Mystery of the Musk Rose' in his *Climbing Roses Old and New.* Basically *R. moshata* is a Himalayan rose but has been cultivated since classical times throughout India and in Mediterranean areas. Again, being a source of attar of roses, the plant was not at the mercy, as far as popularity is concerned, of mere aesthetics; being grown commercially meant propagation in considerable quantity and hence the greater likelihood of its becoming natualized, which it did in various areas of the Mediterranean littoral. Unlike the other 'ancestors,' *R. moschata* is not utterly frost hardy – lack of summer ripening of the wood can lead to winter die-back; hence its relatively late appearance in North Europe.

Hakluyt says that *R. moschata* was brought to England from Italy in the entourage of Lord Cromwell. This can be dated 1513 and during that century it developed a considerable popularity, being enjoyed particularly for its evening scent borne upon their air. Parkinson notes how the fragrance is engendered less in the petals than in the stamens. It must be accepted however that Shakespeare's Musk rose at the start of *A Midsummer Night's Dream* –

> I know a bank where the wild thyme blows
> Where oxlips and the nodding violet grows
> Quite over-canopied with luscious woodbine
> With sweet musk roses and with eglantine.

– is not botanically *R. moschata* but the white indigenous *R. arvensis*. This scented scrambler with purplish stems is a part of the English country midsummer-night scene and anyway it is unfair to delve too deeply into the botany of poets, except perhaps that of Erasmus Darwin who, in his 'Botanic Garden', leads with his chin.

But clearly, John Parkinson, whose life overlapped with that of Shakespeare, knew and described a very different plant:

> The Musk Rose, both single and double, rise up oftentimes to a very great height, that it over-groweth any arbour in a garden or being set by an house side to be ten or twelve foote high or more, but more especially the single kinde, with many green farre spread branches, armed with a few great thornes.

The true Musk Rose, from Crispin van de Passe's Hortus Foridus

Of the flowers, single and double, which open at the end of summer and in the autumn he says: 'both of them a very sweete and pleasing smell, resembling Muske'. In the next century Miller described it thus (knowing more roses his words are more comparative):

> This rises with weak stalks to the height of ten or twelve feet, covered with a smooth greenish bark and armed with short strong spines... The leaves are smooth and composed of three pairs of oval spear-shaped lobes, terminating in points ending with an odd one, they are of a light green colour and sawed on the edges; the flowers are produced in large bunches, in the form of umbels, at the end of the branches; these appear in August and continue in succession till the frost stops them; they are white, and have a fine musky odour. There is one with single and another with double flowers of this sort. The stalks of these plants should be placed where they may have support.

And all the early writers comment upon a climbing, late-flowering, distinctively scented white rose. Yet, surprisingly, texts in our own century from Miss Willmott to the *Royal Horticultural Society's Dictionary of Gardening* use this name for a monster summer flowerer which came into cultivation much later. It seemed that the old Musk rose had died out. But fortunately Mr Thomas looked out E. A. Bowles's *My Garden in Summer* written in 1914, where he found that:

> The true and rare old Musk Rose exists here, but in a juvenile state at present, for it is not many years since I brought it as cuttings from the splendid old specimen on The Vicarage, at Bitton, and I must not expect its

> deliciously scented, late in the season flowers before it has scrambled up its wall space.

(The Bitton garden, near Bath, was that of the famous Victorian gardener Canon Ellacombe, a noted rosarian.)

After decades of decline after its owner's death E. A. Bowles's Myddelton House garden near Enfield is now in the care of Lee Valley Parks and is available to the public. In 1963 it was still being maintained after the creator's death and Mr Thomas was able to go and collect material of that 'true and rare old Musk rose'. Surprisingly, the propagating material, taken from what had always been a single rose (some had been used for budding, some for cuttings) produced the following year nothing but double flowers.

The old writers all note how the Musk rose varies between double and single flowers and here, in front of the very person most likely to notice, remark and come to the right conclusions, the plant decided to exhibit both its manifestations. One can only here marvel at the long arm of coincidence or accept with happiness the old saying that, in a horticultural sense at least, God helps those who help themselves.

The real significance, of course, of this elusive rose – because it is not in truth a very exciting plant is itself – is that, as had been indicated, it has come to be part of other roses by accidental crossing over centuries, particularly with the European red rose, *R. gallica*, to produce the historic *R.* x *bifera* the Autumn Damask. The Musk rose's late-flowering gene in combination produced that second autumn blooming which was the joy of the ancients who grew it. As is shown later, it is also a part of the Provence or Cabbage roses: it also reoccurs much later as a tiny part of the interesting and beautiful garden roses known as the Hybrid Musks.

The final, fifth ancestor is described by Alice Coats as 'an impostor – an upstart no more than four centuries of age – compared to the twenty at least of its companions' – *R. centifolia.*

The hundred-leaved (that is, hundred-petalled) roses of the ancients extolled by Theophrastus and Pliny are forms of *R. damascena*, where even if a perfect continuum of records is not available, at least the gaps, if the Arabian connection is not neglected, are not impossibly great.

The great confusion here, of course, is Linnaeus's adoption of the name (*Species Plantarum,* 1753) of *R. centifolia*. Although Latin binomials are names not needing to be translated into the vernacular of the reader, the exercise is so involuntary that one is almost bound to interpolate 'hundred-leaved rose' with all the eventual confusion that ensues.

Nothing much seems to be known before the end of the sixteenth century; it was the Musk rose and the Damask that the Elizabethans doted upon. An uncertain reference of about 1580 brings *R. centifolia* into their period: it seems to have come from the East via Austria, but both France and Holland have claims which lead to its names as Dutch or Provence rose. By the early years of the eighteenth century it begins to appear in English nurserymen's catalogues. The common and not entirely complimentary name of Cabbage rose followed later.

Modern cytology suggests the presence of four species in the make-up of *R. centifolia*. These are *R. gallica* and *R. moshcata* – two of the vital five ancestors – with *R. phoenicea* and *R. canina*. And when it is realized what the different pairings of these four species are, *R. gallica* and *R. phoenicea* making the Summer Damask, *R. gallica* and *R. moschata* the Autumn Damask, and *R. canina* being part of *R. alba*, one sees what an amazing amalgam the Cabbage rose is. Not surprisingly, in view of its complicated chromosomal complement and its highly petaloid pattern with consequent staminal reduction, the plant is sexually sterile, though Shepherd states that with the removal of a central ball of petals fertile stamens do become available.

Fortunately, this in no way obviates the likelihood of bud mutation in which the apical cell of a developing shoot produces by chance a genetic change, which may be either the reduction of the normal chromosome number or an unpredictable somatic difference. Such oddities of cell behaviour may, incidentally, be not infrequent, but it is the cell at the extreme tip, which by continual division builds up the whole new shoot, that has to be significantly different to be noticed.

Such a mutation of *R. centifolia* is that which produced the Moss roses. In spite of their being less than 300 years old, to many of us they are the epitome of old-fashioned roses.

The first reference is a somewhat doubtful one from Carcassonne, in south-west France, in the 1690s. This may seem quite late, but it is likely that if botanical writers such as Clusius or Parkinson or Gerard knew the Moss rose, they would have mentioned it. And can it be doubted that Shakespeare or Spenser would not have brought some romantic analogy?

This 'moss' is not just of visual importance, its origin is in the extended oil glands with which many old roses add to their fragrance. In the Moss roses the glands are extended and proliferate all round the calyx, the sepals of which often end in a fringed and mossy manner. It is interesting here to refer to the 'Five Brethren of the Rose' (see page 266) to these greatly enlarged beards. All of this produces an even more than usually fragrant rose which makes it not surprising that the enthusiasm for discovering further Moss roses has been considerable.

It has been suggested that Gerard's 'Velvet Rose' is a Moss. It starts right enough:

> The velvet Rose groweth always very low, like unto the red rose, having his branches covered with a certaine hairy or prickly matter, as fine as haires, yet not so sharp or stiffe that will harm the most tender skin that is: the leaves are like the leaves of the white rose: the flowers grow at the top of the stalks, doubled with some yellow

> thrums in the midst of a deepe and blacke red colour, resembling when the flowers be faded, there follow red berries of crimson velvet, whereupon some have called it the Velvet rose full of hard seeds, wrapped in a downe or woolinesse like the others.

Yet no Moss rose ever produces seeds and it must be concluded that what later extractors have taken to be moss in Gerard's first sentence must refer to a raspberry stem-like bristliness. Gerard's illustration, taken from L'Obel of 1581 (only sixteen of the former's illustrative woodcuts are in fact original) shows a semi-double flower and no sign of moss at all on a thornless stem.

The great Dutch botanist Boerhaave lists a real Moss rose growing in the old Leyden Botanic Garden in 1720, but it is unfortunate indeed that at the celebrated exchange of plants and seeds between John Watts of the Chelsea Physic Garden and Paul Hermann of Leyden in 1684, which initiated the now international botanic garden seed and plant exchange system, no roses are recorded.

However, Chelsea did not have long to wait because Philip Miller, who became the most famous botanical gardener of his time and was in charge at Chelsea for nearly fifty years, says that he first saw a Moss rose in 1727 'in the garden of Dr Boerhaave near Leyden, who was so good as to give me one of the plants'. Miller says in a later edition of his monumental *Gardener's Dictionary*, in referring to the 'Moss Provence Rose,' that while the flowers do resemble the common Provence rose the Moss 'is undoubtedly a distinct species, for although the stalks and shoots are very like those of the Common, yet the plants are very difficult to propagate while the common sort is not'.

He goes on to describe how loath it is to sucker, how difficult to layer and how short-lived grafted plants are if this has to be resorted to. These remarks and his description, 'the footstalks of the flower are of an elegant crimson colour, and have a most agreeable odour,' are those not only of a man who has seen the plant but who has grown it as well.

When in 1722 Sir Hans Sloane (the Lord of the Manor of Chelsea) granted a lease at £5 ($9) a year in perpetuity of the Physic Garden site to the Society of Apothecaries he virtually refounded this historic botanic garden. He stipulated certain conditions to guarantee, as he hoped, that 'it be for ever kept up and maintained by the Company as a physick garden'. One condition was that every year fifty plant specimens, pressed and mounted, should be sent to him for his herbarium collection. This, at his death in 1753, went with all his other cabinets of curiosities to form the nucleus of the British Museum. According to Miss Willmott (1914), among his 3,700 plant specimens is a Moss rose, dated 1735, which Miller sent. This would be the earliest existing specimen although there are a couple of illustrations which predate it by a year or so.

Unfortunately, a search of some of the vast Sloane collections failed to turn up this specimen which presumably Ellen Willmott actually saw. For much of this information we are indebted to Dr C. C. Hurst (1870-1947) who, as one of the original geneticists – for we are apt to forget how recent a science this is – worked on the origins of roses from the 1920s at the University Botanic Garden at Cambridge. His invaluable 'Notes on the Origin and Evolution of our Garden Roses' appeared in the 1941 *Journal of the Royal Horticultural Society:* so original are they, and germane to any discussion of old roses that Mr Graham Thomas republished them in his *The Old Shrub Roses.*

As the eighteenth century progressed, Dr Hurst relates, references to the Moss rose gradually became more frequent. By the mid-century, it has been recorded as growing in four distinct areas of south and west France. Linnaeus, who had missed it in his *Species Plantarum* 1753, classified Miller's Double Red Moss simply as a form of *R. centifolia* in 1762 (Miller at this time was still holding fast to the old Latin phrase-name system for scientific plant names and had not moved on to use Linnaeus's more convenient binominals.) One reference is that the Moss rose was sent to Mme de Genlis in France from Lord Mansfield in England as a new introduction from north to south. While we now know this to be untrue, it does indicate that the plant, at least away from specialist gardens, was still virtually unknown to most people.

By the turn of the century, several forms had occurred, by further bud mutation, of plants of the original Carcassome Moss mutation; very importantly, this had occurred in places where they were noticed and propagated. It must be remembered that, without the keen observation of various early rosarians, all the forms derived from the Cabbage rose, Moss or otherwise, would have been transient phenomena, for *R. centifolia* is sterile. 'White Moss' appeared in 1788, 'Blush Moss' in 1789 and the 'Striped Moss' was discovered in 1790. The rest must wait, as indeed did they, for discussion of the nineteenth-century rose.

But the Cabbage rose did not restrict its sporting to the production of the mossy variant, and several interesting accounts have come down to us which describe its appearance and subsequent propagation. The typical form, which is seen in so many seventeenth-century Dutch flower pictures – often depicted with such realism that one feels they could be picked off the canvas or panel – is a demurely drooping flower. The weight of the full flower on the peduncle (which Miller calls the footstalk) and the combined weight of many blossoms on one bough provide an atmosphere of almost languorous luxuriance.

The colour is a delicate shell-pink, deepening toward the centre of the tight 'hundred-leaves' and the scent is particularly strong, which, when we remember its parentage, is not surprising. The petals are held together by a broad-spreading, persistent calyx.

The two earliest recorded Centifolia variants are both floral miniatures. Hurst suggested that the 'Rose de Meaux' was probably named to commemorate Doménique Séguier, Bishop of Auxerre from 1631 to 1637, when he was translated to the see of Meaux. As Séguier was a noted patron of horticulture in his time and a keen rose grower it is agreeable conjecture. Neither Linnaeus nor Miller mentions the 'Rose de Meaux' but that it predated them in its own country is clear. Its lovely buds open to form almost flat flowers an inch across, of typical Cabbage rose colour. Flowering time is rather in advance of the type.

The 'Rose de Meaux,' though dwarf, has the usual light green Centifolia leaves on a typically open bush, but its other dwarf contemporary is darker leaved and of upright habit. This had been called *R. centifolia parvifolia*, known among several other names as 'Pompon de Burgogne.' Mr Thomas exactly describes its rosette-like flowers as being 'of dark Tyrian pink suffused with claret and purple, with paler centres'. The first known illustration of this old rose is in a work of the botanist Tabernaemontanus in 1664.

A third pre-nineteenth-century Cabbage rose is 'Unique Blanche,' the 'White Provence Rose.' Variations in the story of its origin are several but all begin in the 1770s in Norfolk or Suffolk.

The earliest written version of the story seems to be that of Henry Andrews, 1805:

> Its introduction in 1777 was entirely accidental, through the medium of the late Mr. Greenwood, Nurseryman, a great admirer and collector of Roses who, in an excursion which he usually made every summer was passing the front garden of Mr. Richmond, a baker near Needham in Suffolk. There he perceived the present charming plant, where it had been placed by a carpenter who found it in a hedge on the contiguous premises of a Dutch merchant, whose old mansion he was repairing. Mr. Greenwood, requesting a little cutting of it, received from Mr. Richmond of the whole plant, when Mr. Greenwood, in return for a plant so valuable, presented him with an elegant silver cup with the Rose engraved upon it …[1]

With so much circumstantial evidence it might seem likely that other accounts would follow closely. But no, the same Mr Greenwood enjoyed his discovery also in Norfolk in July 1775 ('when riding very leisurely along the road') in the garden of a mill. He gave the old lady there a guinea for a flower, buying the whole plant a year later for £5 ($9) and sending this fortunate Schone Müllerin (a more romantic recipient than a baker) a 'superb silver Tankard, etc. to the amount of £60' ($105).

Interesting too is the knowledge, if indeed it be true, that Mr Greenwood, nurseryman, bulked up the stock from his original bud stick and then the stock plant itself to be able to sell 1,200 plants at a guinea a time three years later. This is as significant for the history of the rose as it was for the fortunate Mr Greenwood's bank account, because it makes it quite clear that there was a keen market for a new plant at the considerable price of a guinea – £15 ($27) might be a comparable figure today and dreadful charges of profiteering would be brought against a nurseryman trying to obtain it. The further and more important point is a social one: 1778 was the peak of the landscape school of garden design when, if most texts are to be believed, the recognizable garden was being irrevocably swept away from the house and the park brought up to its very doors. Lancelot Brown and his school had decreed (following William Kent, who, it is said, 'leapt the fences and saw that all nature was a garden') the use only of grass and native trees – though Cedars of Lebanon were permitted to provide a contrast in shape and texture. Flowers were banished out of sight to the enclosed kitchen garden, roses with them.

Yet even so important a country house as Nuneham Park in Oxfordshire, which had been built to demonstrate Lord Harcourt's perfect taste (he had been tutor to the young King George III), had its flower garden. This was the brainchild of his son, later the second Earl Harcourt who, with the advice of William Mason, laid out a Rousseauesque garden. With the ideas of *La Nouvelle Héloise* and the Noble Savage in mind, an informal, mock-naturalist garden was made of which roses and honeysuckle were inevitably vital parts.

With such ideas gaining ground, the time was ripe for flower growing even in fashionable circles; in unfashionable circles flower growing had never entirely fallen out of favour. In gardens of the 'curious,' to use a contemporary term which was not then one of opprobrium, the unusual specimen had always been sought. Similarly, on a large scale and perhaps with more scientific overtones, the Botanic Gardens at Oxford, Chelsea, later Cambridge and William Curtis's at Lambeth had all acquired their collections. The botanic garden ethos, if so it may be called, was clearly given a boost by Princess Augusta's garden at Kew, which by the end of the eighteenth century was beginning, with Sir Joseph Banks in charge, to take on the air of a national institution.

Into this atmosphere then, if not directly into these particular gardens, came the discoveries of travellers from abroad who brought back plants rather by chance; soon collectors were being sent out by wealthy patrons to this particular end. Roses of course were among the finds.

North America had early produced two fine roses for European gardens. *R. virginiana* (Miller's rather confusing name, as it does not grow wild so far south) comes from Newfoundland down to Pennsylvania and was the first American species certainly to cross the Atlantic in the early years of the seventeenth century. Its fine showering habit and brilliant shining leaves, which justify Ehret's name of *R. lucida*, seem not to have been very highly thought of by Philip Miller: however he introduced in 1768 the even lovelier double hybrid known as 'St Mark's Rose'. In Venice this plant is expected to flower on the saint's name-day, April 25. It is also known as the 'Rose d'Amour.'

'It is quite an achievement, I think,' says Mr Thomas of another species, 'for a wild rose of China to become so established and naturalized in the United States that it has acquired the name of the "Cherokee Rose" and has, moreover, been accepted as the State flower of Georgia.' This enormous rose with flowers rather like a Romneya was described first in 1705 as a native of southern China and is said to have been first cultivated in Britain at Chelsea in 1759. Presumably it soon crossed the Atlantic from east to west because in 1803 Michaux (whose name, *R. laevigata*, it carries) found it romping to the tops of trees. Such was its profusion then and now that there are still hopeful suggestions that this rose might be truly native to North America, a remnant of the flora shared with Asia when a land-bridge still existed.

Although neither made anything of mark in eighteenth-century gardens in Britain or on the Continent, two important climbing roses were found which are now highly regarded. The first of these is the Macartney Rose, *R. bracteata*. It was brought from China in 1793 by Lord Macartney, who was on a diplomatic mission. Unfortunately it has never become at all common in Britain as it needs more warmth than it normally gets there. But on a suitable wall it is a magnificent plant with great white, gold-centred flowers surrounded by the brilliant green bracts which give its name. The whole has an extraordinary heraldic appearance. This is combined with a heavily fruity scent and virtually evergreen foliage. The stout fifteen-foot-long shoots are wickedly armed and careless pruners should beware: as with the so-called 'Australian bush-lawyers' (species of *Rubus*) it is not as easy to get out of its clutches as it is to get in. For this reason, in certain southern states of the USA, *R. bracteata* has become something of a pest, growing hugely and rooting as it goes.

The second late eighteenth-century addition to our complement of roses also came from China and, although the first introduction is quite well documented, it took from 1796 to1909 to flower. Now, while *R. banksiae*, for this is it, does take a few years to settle down to flower well, to take over a century is excessive. The story is that Robert Drummond brought it from the Far East whence he had accompanied his brother, Admiral Drummond. The rose was planted at the family home, Megginch Castle in Scotland. There it grew but, lacking hardiness, was so frequently cut down by the frost that it had failed to develop the three-or-more-year-old thornless stems which are necessary for it to flower. Eventually, cuttings from this specimen were grown in a garden in the French Riviera: this, Mr Thomas asserts, was the first time the single wild white form of Lady Banks' Rose flowered in Europe.

It obtained its name, however, from another form and another introduction, but close enough to the turn of the eighteenth and nineteenth centuries to make it permissible to mention it here. One of the earliest professional plant collectors was William Kerr, whom the Royal Society sent to China in 1803. He brought from a Canton garden the double white form of this rose. It flowered near Kew in 1807 and was named after the wife of the Royal Gardens' director, Sir Joseph Banks. Subsequently, first double and then single yellow forms were discovered: all are most lovely plants, especially enjoying the warmth of a Mediterranean climate. To see the soft yellow forms cascading out of high olive trees in association with wisteria, in Corfu for instance, is a magnificent sight.

But Europe had to wait a long time before such displays could be enjoyed. We see these three centuries from 1500 as a period when only gradually were the horizons of the garden widened to encompass developments of knowledge, technology and, in parallel, a vastly increased complement of plants.

Gerard's famous *Herball* of 1597 can be seen as just such a transitional work: it is in the shadow of the dark ages yet struggling to get into the light. He refers to the past in such a context in the following passage:

> The yellow rose which (as divers do report) was by art so coloured, and altered from his first estate by grafting

> upon a Broome stalke; whereby (say they) it doth not only change his colour, but his smell and force. But for my part (having found the contrarie by mine owne experience) cannot be induced to beleeve the report; for the roots and offsprings of this rose have brought forth yellow roses such as the main stocke or mother bringeth out, which event is not to be seen in all other plants that have been grafted. Moreover, the seeds of the yellow roses have brought forth yellow …

Having knocked that bit of medieval nonsense on the head. Gerard goes on to illustrate and describe what he calls *R. lutea multiplex*. It is, he says, very uncommon, not surprisingly because 'it seldome fully shewes it self about London, where it is kept in our chiefe gardens as a prime raritie.'

This clearly is what is now called *R. hemisphaerica*, still rarer, still difficult to flower at all well – in a dull summer hardly a flower opens – but until the middle of the nineteenth century the only double yellow rose known.

It should be mentioned here that, while Gerard grew in his Holborn garden at the end of the sixteenth century both *R. foetida* and *R. foetida bicolor* (Austrian Yellow and Austrian Copper), it is best to discuss their contributions to the potential of the rose in another chapter (see page 156). Enough here, to explain the name, is to quote a contemporary of Gerard's, Dalechamps (*Historia Plantarum*, 1587) in Miss Willmott's translation:

> Its odour is unpleasant, nature did wrong in depriving such a beautiful flower of the perfume which it should have had in common with other Roses, for had it only given forth a sweet scent, it would not have ranked among the least of beautiful flowers.

Perhaps we may consider that the eglantine with its scented flowers and leaves makes up for this heinous rose offence.

Gradually, then, with new species from the Orient and the New World, with the gathering together of the roses from European hedgerows, and with the selection of different forms of all types, the world of the rose begins to open up like one of its own prize blooms. The following century was to see a full blossoming.

[1] H. C. Andrews, *Roses,* 1805-1828

A Dutch allegorical print: falling rose petals reflect the transience of life

CHAPTER 5

GREAT ROSE GARDENS

Roses cannot exist in isolation and the evolution of roses in cultivation has both affected and been affected by changing styles and tastes in garden design. Rose gardens in the full sense of that phrase – that is, a garden devoted principally to this one genus – are of remarkably recent date when seen in the context of several millennia of rose-growing. The credit for 'inventing' the rose garden seems to go to the Empress Josephine of France at her Château de Malmaison in the first decade of the nineteenth century.

Before this, although good garden descriptions are rare, we see – from Pompeian wall frescoes to paintings of the early eighteenth century – roses as part of the garden scene. They may appear predominant in works dedicated to Venus or – in another, yet related, context – to the Virgin Mary; but here, as we have seen, the rose arbours and putti-held swags are aids to the observer's symbolic appreciation of the work. They can seldom be taken as definite representations of medieval or Renaissance rose growing. Similarly, the rose-obsessed imagery in the early illustrations to the *Roman de la Rose* may show a series of apparent rose gardens, but it is unwise to take them too literally. For just as a garden is itself one conception of paradise, non-topographical illustrations of gardens compound idealization upon idealization.

Yet we can at least assume that the painters concerned based their flights of artistic fancy upon a basis of current fact which we can check against contemporary representations of gardens in herbals and the like. Early gardens are invariably enclosed – a society needs to feel both physically and psychologically secure before it can open its mind and its gardens to the world at large. So it was not until the great change of taste was brought to a full flowering by the mid-eighteenth century landscape school, reacting against enclosures and extravagant formality, that gardens became a part of the world – albeit a contrived one. Ironically, for that period 'flowering' is a grossly inaccurate word. Fashionable eighteenth-century landscape gardening banished all flowers from the immediate view as the park was brought up to the windows of the equally fashionable Palladian house. The ideal scene became a classical temple – be it house, mausoleum or Protestant church behind the pillared portico – in an idealized reinterpretation of the Roman *campagna*. There was no place for the rose.

Fortunately, this did not mean that no roses were grown in the eighteenth century. On the contrary, we have already seen how the range of roses available steadily increased and nurseries had no difficulty, it seems, in selling special novelties for considerable sums. Early nurserymen's catalogues are rare, but the Osborn collection at York University Library has that of William

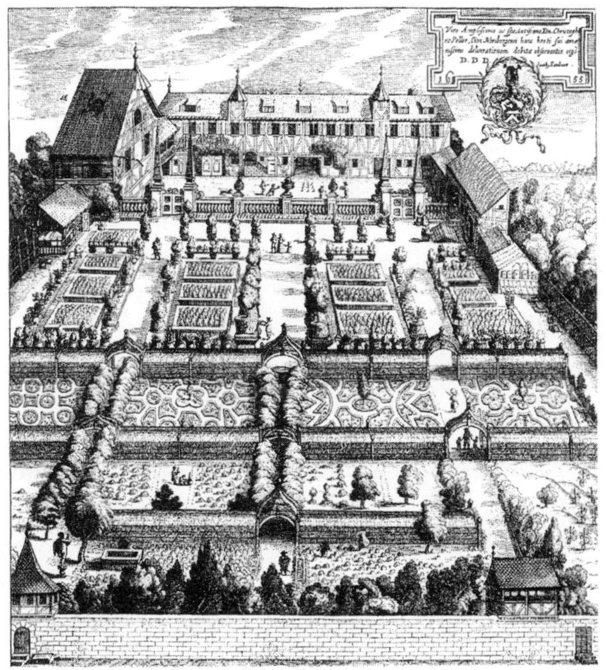

An entirely enclosed and inward looking garden – that of Christoph Peller, Nuremburg, drawn in 1655

Joyce of Gateshead, County Durham, dated 1754. Thirty-two roses are listed and priced. Among the cheapest are Rosa Munda *(sic)*, the Monthly and 'Cabbage or Province' at 4d; 'Moss Province' at 2s is the most expensive, while 'Dutch 100 leaved' and 'Blush Belgick' are 1s and 'Double Yellow' and 'White Cluster or Musk' cost 1s 6d. But at the houses of the great, the walled kitchen garden was their place – to provide copious cut flowers for indoor decoration. Philip Miller, writing of sweetbrier, makes this abundantly clear:

> The flowers being single, are not valued, but the Branches of the shrubs are cut to intermix with Flowers to place in Basons to adorn Halls, Parlours etc. in the Spring of the year, the scent of this plant being agreeable to most persons.

In one sense, therefore, roses continued to be part of the enclosed garden which we see depicted from earlier times. There the roses are tied flat on walls, they are used to divide areas by being trained on trellises, they are grown as bushes and even taken up to be standards with a wheel-like contraption for the training of umbrella-shaped heads. All the components, it would seem, of the modern rose garden – but without its exclusivity. Where roses are depicted they are neither massed nor do they grow alone. There is invariably a clear indication of their being a part of a miscellany of plants – shrubs, herbaceous things, annuals, bulbs, fruit trees and bushes with an almost cottage garden randomness. Of hedges it was written:

> Everyman taketh what liketh him best
> as either privet alone or sweet Bryar,
> and whitehorn interlaced together,
> and Roses of one, two or more sorts
> placed here and there amongst them.[1]

In cottage gardens and the gardens of collectors, roses and other flowers continued to be grown thus throughout the seventeenth and eighteenth centuries. High fashion decreed, firstly, geometrical patterns which, in their most extreme form, made any living plants unnecessary and, secondly, that garden and landscape were one.

The gardens which maintained the largest collection of roses (and of most other plants) were the Botanic or Physic – the terms were synonymous – gardens. These were set up from the 1450s, beginning in Pisa and Padua, to accompany university schools of medicine. That they were concerned with *Materia Medica* is obvious, but that only tells half the story. They were, as now, scientific institutions devoted to the extension of plant-based study. Hence they were apt to grow as many plants as possible for demonstration and comparison; they also served as centres for propagation and distribution.

The *Catalogus Plantarum Horti Medici Oxoniensis* of 1648 lists twenty-one roses. Ten years later, in what was then headed *Catalogus Horti Botanici Oxoniensis*, it held thirty-two different roses including *R. alba*, *R. semperflorens* and *R. damascena*.

Almost a century later, Philip Miller's *Gardener's Dictionary* (2nd edition of 1735) listed forty-six, and with them detailed descriptions of their cultivation. No doubt he grew most of them at the Chelsea Physic Garden of which he was curator. But the *Dictionary*, although described, it is said, by Linnaeus as '*Non erit Lexicon Hortulanorum, sed etiam Botanicorum*' (Not merely a dictionary of horticulture, but a dictionary of botany') was concerned to bring effective horticultural techniques to a wider public than the purely botanical. Again, the effort is to obtain early cut-flowers for the house, not to provide, with glass before and manure behind, an attractive garden scene:

> It is proper to plant some of the monthly Roses near a warm Wall, which will occasion their Budding at least three weeks or a month before those in the open air: and if you give them the Help of a Glass before them, it will bring their flowers much forwarder, especially where Dung is plac'd to the Backside of the wall (as is practis'd in raising Early Fruits). By this method I have seen fair Roses of this kind blown in *February*, and they may be brought much sooner where people are curious this way.

What NATURE ſparing gives, or half denies.
See! healthfull INDUSTRY at large ſupplies.
See! in BRITANNIA'S Lap profuſely pours.
While heaven-born SCIENCE ſwells th'increaſing Store.
Ecce! ferunt Pueri Calathis Tibi Lilia plenis. VIRG.

Frontispiece to Miller's Gardener's Dictionary

Fortunately, gardeners are and always have been 'curious this way.' There have always been some who refused to be slaves of fashion. We have only to look at the charming drawings and watercolours of Thomas Robins (1716-1802) to see such originality during the period when the landscape school was at its peak of popularity.

Without Robins we would have almost no visual record that there were alternatives, and floral alternatives at that. Working mainly in and around Bath and in Shropshire he displays:

> A rococo artist's vision of what must be regarded as rococo gardens, and there is no doubt that Robins was peculiarly drawn to this ephemeral world of chinoiserie kiosks, root houses and arbours, grottoes and hermitages, fret fences and palings, rockwork cascades, Gothic temples and all the whimsical knick-knackery of these gardens of delight.[2]

Robins's gardens are not cottage gardens in any sense, but they do have flowers in them and, inevitably, among them there are roses. So are they depicted in the rococo scrollwork which frames his happy scenes.

Perhaps an earlier work with which Philip Miller was associated has a connection with rose-growing of this type. A Society of London Gardeners was formed in the 1720s, consisting mainly of nurserymen concerned to popularize their stock, and Miller and Fairchild, both members, brought out in 1730 a *Catalogus Plantarum* of 'Trees & Shrubs, both exotic & domestic, which are hardy enough to bear the cold of our Climate in the Open Air.' Forty-three roses are listed as being available to the public and recommended for:

> being intermix't with flowering trees & shrubs in small wilderness quarters afford the most agreeable prospect of any of the Flowering Trees and the great variety of Sorts do continue flowering at least three months. They are all very hardy & may be planted in the openest places.

A further, though very differently motivated, instance can be cited of eighteenth-century rose-growing. In the 1750s the first Earl Harcourt, the highly correct Governor to the Prince of Wales, and later, when his charge acceded to the throne as George III, Lord Chamberlain, built a Palladian villa at Nuneham Courtenay in Oxfordshire. Overlooking the Thames and within view of the spires and domes of Oxford, the site exactly fitted what Palladio himself had advocated as the ideal situation for a villa:

> … advantageous and delicious as can be desired, being seated on a hillock of most easy ascent, at the foot of which runs a navigable river and on the other side surrounded by several hills that seem to form an amphitheatre.

By removing the nearby village the Earl was able to create a suitable classical landscape to surround his villa and the ideal scene was, for the time, complete. His son, however, had odd egalitarian ideas (though these did not survive his accession to his father's title, his own middle age and his wife who wished to go to Court).

Lord Nuneham took the philosophy of Jean-Jacques Rousseau as an ideal way of life and indeed tried to put some of it into practice in his own behaviour. But in the context of this book the significance is that, in 1771, he and the poet William Mason laid out what is considered by many to be the first informal flower garden in England and probably in the western world. It was (and to some extent happily still is), in its attempt to actually create Julie's garden as Rousseau described it in his *La Nouvelle Héloise*, both a romantic and a sentimental garden. The words are used of course in their original meanings.

Mason's garden at Nuneham was secluded and enclosed, as with early rose gardens. By a Doric gate a bust of Flora was inscribed with these lines from the *Romaunt of the Rose*:

Here springs the violet all newe,
And fresh periwinkle riche of hewe
And Flowis yalowe, white and rede
Such planti grew there ner in mede;
Full gai is all the ground and queint,
And pondrid, as men had it peint …

And other verses to encourage suitable sentiment occurred on rocks, grotto, bower (wallpapered with a pattern of roses and batons) and urn. Such artifice was not original but the irregular flower beds, the insouciant mixture of native and exotic plants, and the encouragement of honeysuckle and roses to scramble up the trees certainly was. We can see it as a conception which, horticulturally speaking, was a hundred years before its time. So too, perhaps, was this attitude to Walter Clarke, the resident florist, recorded on a great stone near the grotto. The lines are by William Whitehead, the poet laureate, who knew Clarke, and the garden well:

> Twas here he fell, not far remov'd
> Has earth received him in her breast.
> Still fast beside the scenes he lov'd
> in holy ground his relics rest …
> Each clambering woodbine, flaunting rose
> Which round yon bower be taught to wave
> With every fragrant breeze that blows
> Shall lend a wreath to bind his grave.

Although Mason's garden was greatly admired – Horace Walpole, a frequent visitor, called it 'a quintessence of nosegays' – as a garden style it was overshadowed by the grandeur of the landscape school of which 'Capability' Brown was the prime exponent. That the two styles were not antagonistic (for the former could be easily hidden in the latter) is clear from the fact that Brown was brought in not only to work on the park at Nuneham but to remodel the house as well. The time was not ripe; but it is significant that Humphrey Repton, who took up Brown's mantle on the latter's death in 1783, increasingly used flowers adjacent to the house. Recent research shows he was by no means alone in this.[3]

In the charming sketches of his own small garden at Hare Street in Essex (Repton's irresistible technique was to draw before and after scenes of gardens to be improved, the one superimposed upon the other), he shows bush roses and others trained up a tripod. One of his last commissions was in 1814 for the Earl of Bridgwater at Ashbridge in Hertfordshire. Here Repton was not required to landscape a vast park, but to concentrate upon gardens near to the house. Here he designed what he termed a 'rosarium' of some extent.

Repton's watercolour sketch views a low trellis fence surrounding the rose garden from the rose-clad arches of an elegant gazebo. Further arches rise above the trellis fence, each is tightly bound with roses. The garden inside is like a great daisy laid out on the ground: seventeen rose-bed petals and a high central fountain spilling into a basin.

While Repton's Ashbridge rosarium must be one of the earliest full-scale rose gardens in England (of which only traces remain), in France one particular rose garden had already enjoyed a decade of great acclaim. This was at the Château de Malmaison, home of the Empress Josephine.

The story of Marie-Josèphe Rose Tascher de la Pagerie has been often related but never ceases to exercise its fascination. Fiction could do no better that it is worth retelling. Born in Martinique in the French West Indies, she was sent to relations in Paris at the age of sixteen and a year later (in 1780) married Alexandre, Vicomte de Beauharnais. During the Terror both were imprisoned and the Vicomte went to the guillotine in 1794, a fate which his wife narrowly avoided. Josephine retired in some poverty to Croissy but soon attracted the attention of a rising young general of the Revolutionary Army, Napoleon Buonaparte. They were married in 1796.

Buonaparte had, it seems, decided that they should buy a country house and, while he was away on his Egyptian campaign in 1799, Josephine bought in her own name (and with borrowed money) the Château de Malmaison, near Choisy, and its estate of 650 acres. At the end of that same year, the *coup d'etat* made Buonoparte First Consul of the Republic; five years later he crowned himself Emperor and the short reign of Empress Josephine began. Although she had had two children by M de Beauharnais, Josephine appeared unable to produce the heir to the dynasty Buonoparte hoped to found and he divorced her 'for reasons of state' in 1810. Napoleon's defeat and Josephine's death followed only four years later.

The bones of this classic rags-to-riches story cannot do justice to the extraordinary state of world events of which Malmaison was, for some years, the centre. In spite of the Revolution, and the almost constant wars waged during Josephine's time at Malmaison, no reading of the domestic doings at the château gives any impression that one civilization, that of the *ancien régime,* had fallen and another was being created.

The simple façade of the château dates mainly from 1737 and harmonizes with the 'English' landscape garden on the west side which Josephine and her English gardener, Howatson, began at once to lay out at the turn of the century. For this the Hammersmith nursery of Lee and Kennedy supplied much of the plant material: bills of £2,600 and £700 (perhaps £75,000 or $135,000 in modern money) in 1811 are recorded. John Kennedy had a special passport to enable him to cross with plants from the one warring country to the other and it is said that if any ship taken as prize carried plants or seeds destined for Malmaison, it was to be sent on its way immediately by orders of the British Admiralty.

Rare plants thus came from all over the world to build up what quickly became a noted botanical collection; between 1803 and 1814, over 200 species flowered there for the first time in France. Heathers from the Cape of Good Hope were an early exotic specialism and other groups which Josephine popularized included camellias, dahlias and pelargoniums.

But it is for her roses that we particularly remember the Empress and the Château de Malmaison. In spite of this almost legendary fame it is sad that no full contemporary list exists of the roses grown there. Almost a century after Josephine's death, the *roseraie*, having soon fallen into neglect, was replanted under the supervision of Jules Gravereaux (the château had become property of the nation in 1903) who worked upon what sources were available. He was able to show that, among others, Josephine grew 167 Gallicas, twenty-seven Centifolias, twenty-two Chinas, nine Damasks, eight Albas, four Spinosissimas, three Luteas and a dozen further species including *Rr. moschata, carolina* and *setigera.* Of these, Gravereaux was able to trace almost 200 still then in cultivation.Conscious hybrdizing had also swelled the numbers and Malmaison can be seen as the base from which the early French predominance in rose growing sprang. It was to last, as has already been shown, for almost the whole of the nineteenth century.

As Josephine is important in the stimulation of rose-growing so is one other pre-eminent. It was her selection of Pierre-Joseph Redouté (1759-1840) to paint her plant collections which ensured his fame and, at the same time, encapsulated hers. Between 1802 and 1816 his eight folios of *Les Liliacées* were published, consisting of 486 coloured plates, and dedicated to the Empress. In 1817 the first parts of *Les Roses* appeared. These won the immediate public acclaim which Redouté's roses (the very phrase brings immediate images to mind) have never lost. One hundred and seventy of Josephine's roses are so immortalized.

Malmaison, where the Empress Josephine assembled her famous collection of roses

In some ways Malmaison today must disappoint; how can such a legend remain alive? Externally the château itself is just as Josephine left it, even to the wooden porch in the shape of a campaign tent which serves as a main entrance. Inside, furnishing and decoration the height of 'Empire' fashion is charming and elegant yet not without a certain exhausting bombast, with its emphasis upon victors' laurel wreaths newly gilt and other motifs of military success. By contrast the *jardin anglais* outside possess a gentle melancholy and the small *roseraie* does not try to compete. A few of Josephine's varieties are grown and, suitably, some beds of 'Souvenir de la Malmaison'. This, of course, is a rose which the Empress could never have known. It had been sent unnamed to Malmaison in 1843 and given its evocative title by the Grand Duke of

Russia who visited and obtained plants for the Imperial Garden at St Petersburg. There is a suitability in the connection between this lovely Bourbon rose and Josephine herself, both having originated in French tropic isles.

Malmaison's present little rose garden dates only from 1920, and while keen rosarians are apt to deplore the discrepancy between a grand past and meaner present, it is unrealistic to expect so transitory a thing as a rose garden to survive the changing fashions and inevitable neglect of nearly two centuries. It is better to visit Malmaison on a sunny morning in early spring (before even Josephine's roses would have shown their first buds) and, having felt the First Empire flavour of the interior and been suitably surprised at the informal 'English' landscape from the west front, walk back down the carriage drive to imagine what Redouté beauties might soon be in flower.

To put flesh upon these recreative thoughts, other rose gardens in Paris or its environs must be seen, at L'Hay les Roses (the 'Roseraie de l'Hay' of that splendid rugosa hybrid and of 'Rose à Parfum de l'Hay') and at Bagatelle; the latter has the more interesting history.

On the west side of the Bois de Boulogne is an area which, in the eighteenth century, several members of the French royal family and their favourites used for the building of discreet and rural hideouts, away from the rigours of Court formality. Bagatelle is one of these.

The original house was built in 1720 by the Duc d'Estrées, the accommodating husband of the delightful and flirtatious Lucie Félicité. In 1772 the property was sold to the Comte d'Artois, brother of the King Louis XVI, and he obtained possession in 1775. By then the Duchesse d'Estrées's little house was in a ruinous condition and M d'Artois decided to rebuild entirely. The manner of this fitted perfectly into the definition of a bagatelle as a toy, a plaything.

The Comte had accepted from Queen Marie Antoinette a wager of 100,000 *livres* that he could not have his new building ready for a fête planned several weeks hence, when the Court was to return from Choisy to Versailles. In a letter to the Queen's mother, Empress Maria-Teresa of Austria, the Comte de Mercy-Argenteau described with disapproval how M d'Artois won his bet.

On 21 September, 1777, work began and, with up to nine hundred men working day and night, encouraged by music and in the light of torches, a new Bagatelle was completed on 26 November. Only sixty-four days had elapsed. What especially concerned M. de Mercy-Argenteau was that, in order to obtain building materials at such short notice, M d'Artois ordered the Garde Suisse to requisition any suitable booty travelling to or from Paris. Immediate payment for such high-handed action did not soothe enraged opinion and perhaps we can see, with hindsight, the charming Bagatelle was forging another nail for the coffin of the *ancien régime*.

The gardens followed. In order to maintain the height of fashion the Comte d'Artois engaged Thomas Blaikie to create a suitable *jardin anglais*. This is well documented in his *Journal of a Scottish Gardener.*

> Monday, 21st December 1778, arrived in Paris. Having seen M Belanger [Alexandre Belanger, architect of Bagatelle], I examine the grounds. There is only some mediocre woodland. He agreed to give me the number of men necessary to finish the gardens in three years.
> Wednesday, 30th December 1778. Began on the gardens of Bagatelle, starting with the wood in front of the pavillion, having cut the trees to open a lawn in company with M Boras, Inspecteur des Bâtiments, but he was surprised to see me plan out the garden without a line! He did not come back.

In fact Blaikie completed his contract in half the time.

> 20th May, 1780. The Count gave a fête at Bagatelle for the King and Queen and the Court which happened to be at La Muette (a nearby château owned by Louis). A splendid military band played upon a stage in a glade during which those invited walked round to admire the gardens.

Bagatelle remained a social centre for the Court until the Revolution in 1789. Three months after the storming of the Bastille the Comte d'Artois fled to Turin and went into an exile that was to last for twenty-four years when he at last returned to Bagatelle.

Toward the end of the Terror, the grounds become available to the public as they have been off and on ever since. The Commune de Neuilly warned:

> Citizens who walk in the Bagatelle must touch nothing and behave decently on pain of being detained and brought before the authorities.

Having been from 1832 the property of Englishmen (principally the Marquis of Hertford and his illegitimate son Richard Wallace – the founder of the Wallace Collection in London), the estate was finally bought by the City of Paris in 1905.

The celebrated rose garden dated from two years earlier on the site of the meadow which the Marquis set aside as a riding paddock for the sons of Napoleon III. Thus it lies to the south of Lord Herford's Orangery, which happily still fulfils its original function, and is surrounded by the fine trees grouped and planted by Alexander Blaikie.

The design of the *roseraie* is basically that of a formal geometrical parterre where each bed is laid with grass and edged with low box hedges. Vertical points of emphasis are made with topiary obelisks of yew while urns and statuary close vistas near and far.

Up to this point such a description could refer to numbers of real or pastiche late seventeenth-century gardens. But, and here is the difference, at Bagatelle (and at L'Hay les Roses, the other Gravereaux garden of similar date), within the box and within the grass subsidiary beds are cut. Most contain a single standard rose and around the base of each are planted five or six bush roses; such an arrangement permits the juxtaposition of numbers of cultivars in a range of colours that would be unacceptable if not tempered by the green predominance of box and grass.

Iron tripods and long pergolas are furnished with a wide range of climbing forms, all impeccably trained and fiercely pruned to ensure that what is apt to be something of an abandoned plant fits into the formal frame of the parterre design. That it does so is best seen from the little chinoiserie Kiosque de l'Impératrice (the Empress here being the consort of Napoleon III).

At Bagatelle there are some 7,000 roses in almost 700 different forms. These are supplemented by those grown as entries in the '*Concours International des Roses nouvelles de Bagatelle*', an annual competition for new roses which was begun in 1907 and attracts entries from all over the world. These, naturally, are labelled only with a number; elsewhere in the *roseraie*, name, raisers and date of origin accompany each rose grown and make a fine reference collection.

We can see such rose gardens as continuing French nineteenth-century tradition into our own day. Thus it is noteworthy that, just as the English landscape garden replaced so many formal designs of the eighteenth century, so, while the Bagatelle rose garden was being laid out in so traditional a way again across the Channel, a movement was fast developing which recommended using plants, roses included, in quite a different manner. It was led by William Robinson and Gertrude Jekyll, whose own books make clear their beliefs and aims. Robinson's *The English Flower Garden* came out in 1883 and had reached its eighth edition in 1900. Miss Jekyll's *Roses for English Gardens* appeared in 1902. Ellen Willmott's *The Genus Rosa* (1914) showed the range of species and forms which could be used to build up Jekyllian garden pictures.

The English Flower Garden is a gathering together of the skirmishes and full-scale battles which Robinson continually waged against what he called 'all the theatrical gardening of Versailles reproduced in Surrey'. In the following quotations it will be seen that one of Robinson's targets is the use of roses as mere sheets of colour or as rigid architectural material.

> The Rose must go back to the flower garden – its true place, not only for its own sake, but to save the garden from ugliness and hardness, and give it fragrance and dignity of leaf and flower.
>
> And they must come back not only in beds, but in the old ways – over bower and trellis ... not in ugly ways, in Roses stuck – and mostly starving – on the top

> of sticks or standards, or set in raw beds of manure and pruned hard and set thin so as to develop large blooms; but as the bloom is beautiful in all stages and sizes, Roses should be seen closely massed, feathering to the ground, the queen of the flower garden in all ways.

It should not be thought that *The English Flower Garden* is all complaint. On the contrary, the chapter entitled 'The New Rose Garden' offers much sense and good advice. This has been taken up to such an extent that today, almost 100 years later, it is apt to seem a series of truisms, rather than the revolutionary credo it once was.

Miss Jekyll's particular genius lay in appreciating the range and diversity of plants that would thrive in the English climate, and with enormous patience and care, in combining them to achieve the garden pictures she had first envisaged in her mind. Thus with roses she had a genus which offered the diversity that she above all was effective in using. The little Scots Burnet roses 'are charming accompaniments to steps and low balustrades … they might well replace the dull and generally ugly steep slopes of turf that disfigure so many gardens'.

And later, of bigger things:

> Many roses, even some of those that one thinks of as rather stiff bushes … only want the opportunity of being planted on some height as on the upper edge of a retaining wall, to show that they are capable of

> exhibiting quite unexpected forms of growth and gracefulness, for they will fling themselves down the face of the wall and flower all the better for the greater freedom.

We have already seen that the intentional use of established trees as living supports for roses was a feature of Mason's garden at eighteenth-century Nuneham Courtenay. Miss Jekyll made a speciality of this natural scrambling ability of many roses.

> When they begin to grow freely among bushes and trees, if it is desired to led the far-reaching growths one way rather than another, it is easily done with a long, forked stick. It is like painting a picture with an immensely long-handled brush, for with a fourteen foot pole with a forked end one can guide the branches into Yew or Holly or tall Thorn very neatly into such forms of upright spring or downward swag as one pleases.

When we remember that Gertrude Jekyll was trained as a painter, and only turned to gardening at the age of forty as her eyesight began to fail, we can the more appreciate her analogy of painting with a fourteen-foot pole.

What rose gardens should be is also made quite clear in *Roses for English Gardens*. As is what they should not be. Among the 200 illustrations there is one pathetic photograph of a country garden, doubtless someone's pride, with the heavily understated caption: 'The usual Rose beds on a lawn. A kind of rose-garden that may be much improved upon.'

How humbling to have one's roses labelled so for all time; what unfortunate immortality.

The Jekyllian rose garden continues the tradition that we have followed in literature and in fact, as a secluded, enclosed place with many of the roses seen against dark shrubs and trees. The discussion then moves in a surprising direction:

> The wisdom of this treatment (dark evergreen backing) is well-known in all other kinds of gardening, but with the tender colours of so many Roses it has a special value. It should be remembered that a Rose garden can never be called gorgeous, the term is quite unfitting ... the gorgeousness of brilliant bloom, fitly arranged, is for other plants and other portions of the garden; here we do not want the mind distracted from the beauty and delightfulness of the rose.

It will be immediately appreciated that these careful words were written in the era of pre-pelargonidin roses. But her first chapter on 'New Garden Roses' showed that as a practicing garden designer she was willing to keep an open mind and to evaluate the new against both the predominant roses of the time – mainly Hybrid Perpetuals and Hybrid Teas – and the older Gallicas and Damasks,

Albas and Centifolias, whose virtues she continued to uphold during their period of general neglect.

There is, today, no Gertrude Jekyll garden which maintains to the full its original planning and planting. Fortunately, however, there are several gardens where the bones can still be seen. So it is safe to accept Russell Page's tribute and see in the best gardens an attitude and atmosphere for which Miss Jekyll is still responsible:

> I can think of few English gardens made in the last fifty years which do not bear the mark of her teaching, whether in the arrangement of a flower border, the almost habitual association of certain plants or the planting of that difficult passage where the garden merges into wild.[4]

Of noted twentieth-century English gardens there are several which, in their choice and use of plants, are clearly related in this way, but perhaps the finest exemplar is Sissinghurst. It began in a most difficult site and it is a very personal essay in garden making in which roses show, in Miss Jekyll's phrase, 'how they may be most beautifully used'.

The story of Sissinghurst has elements that are as strange and remarkable as those of Bagatelle and Malmaison. And, like the latter, it is mainly the product of a strong and talented woman.

In the spring of 1930, Vita Sackville-West, poet, writer and gardener, first saw the site which she was to transform into one of the famous gardens of the twentieth century. The task which she and her husband Harold Nicolson took on was daunting. Sissinghurst Castle was hardly even a ruin; it was the remains of a ruin. A vast Tudor and Elizabethan house had stood in the site until 1800, when it was almost entirely demolished. From that time until the Nicolsons bought it, the remaining buildings became firstly the parish workhouse and then farmworkers' dwellings. The surroundings were a vast rubbish dump.

> Yet the place caught instantly at my heart and my imagination. I fell in love; love at first sight. I saw what might be made of it. It was Sleeping Beauty's Castle; but a castle running away into sordidness and squalor; a garden crying out for rescue. It was easy to see, even then, what a struggle we should have to redeem it.[5]

Today, nearly three quarters of a century later, the great Tudor tower dominates a garden of controlled luxuriance within the plan which Harold Nicolson created. Plantsman and planner combined to achieve their original agreed aim that there should be 'the strictest formality of design with the maximum informality in planting.' Beneath the soil of Sissinghurst are the foundations of a huge house; above it the garden, while not slavishly following those foundations, resembles just such a house: long axial corridors or walks with smaller garden 'rooms' leading off. And, as with the rooms in a house, those garden rooms have particular roles.

The great pink brick walls which still stood 'cried out for a tumble of Roses and Honeysuckle, Figs and Vines.' This was seen at once. Today roses in particular are a speciality of Sissinghurst. In the White Garden, north of the tower, are beds of 'Iceberg' and in the centre a vast bower of *R. longicuspis*. This is one of the many roses E. H. Wilson introduced from north-west China in the early years of this century.

On the other side of the tower is the Rose Garden with numbers of old-fashioned roses in the arrangement and an ambience that, to some extent, gives them this group name. But though there are early Gallicas (such as the striped 'Rosa Mundi'), Albas and Centifolias, newer Hybrids and certain species are found here as well. The important thing is that they should associate well together and with the other plants, herbaceous and shrubby, with which they share the beds and walls. This profusion of growth backed by walls and the great yew rondel gives and entirely different meaning to the often rather restrictive notion of a 'rose-garden.'

At Sissinghurst roses are everywhere: 'Allen Chandler' in the tower courtyard; 'Mme Alfred Carrière' covers one wall of the south cottage, 'Park-direktor Riggers' and the near-black 'Souvenir du Docteur Jamain' are also there. The latter V. Sackville-West rescued from near oblivion and it is now available again. Sissinghurst owes much in its design and use of plants to Lawrence Johnston's Hidcote Manor in Gloucestershire, so it is apt that the rose which bears his name and 'Le Rêve', a sister seedling, should be in the Cottage Garden over which Harold Nicolson took particular pains. (These two roses share a Hybrid Perpetual x Persian Yellow parentage.)

In the orchard, old apple trees offer support to more roses which, having been helped up, now cascade from the branches. Further on, round the foot of an octagonal gazebo, built as a memorial to Harold Nicolson by his son Nigel Nicolson, which looks across the moat over miles of Kentish Weald, is an ancient Gallica. This is one plant which was inherited with the garden and is now known as 'Sissinghurst Castle'.

Something of this same atmosphere of the paradise garden is obtained from other gardens where roses in a controlled yet encouraged profusion make a principal contribution to the scene. Gardens as diverse and as far apart as Ninfa near Rome (this too is built over and around ruins, but of a whole town rather than a single house) and Mainau, an island on Lake Constance. In the nineteenth century the latter was the summer palace of the House of Baden and the gardens, which enjoy an enviably equable climate, include a luxuriant rose garden.

We have seen how, through changing tastes and the prodigious efforts of hybridists to produce ever newer roses, many of the older forms were until quite recently on the verge of extinction even if they had not quite attained that unenviable stage. Fortunately, through the efforts of a few people in first finding and propagating old roses, and then through exhaustive detective work discovering their names, a fine selection of 'old-fashioned' roses is now available to us.

These are nowhere better seen than in what was an old kitchen garden at Mottisfont Abbey in Hampshire. This too, like Sissinghurst, is a property of the National Trust whose garden consultant was Graham Thomas, the foremost expert and champion of old roses. Mr Thomas's own collection of roses came to Mottisfont. The present author has already described this lovely garden:

> Through a door in the high brick wall the visitor is suddenly transported (so long as he goes at the right time of year) into a garden of idealised late-nineteenth-century or Edwardian lushness. At least that is the atmosphere there. It is in fact, in its present form only five years old ... Although the intended collection is not quite complete, towards 300 different forms of roses are already here, providing in June an unsurpassed experience of fragrance and colour. Here are the ancestral species and ancient hybrids, the Portlands, Boubons, tea roses and hybrid perpetuals. Because, however, modern hybrid tea roses are excluded, the range of colours is softer and gentler and altogether more in keeping with an English country garden, however grand.[6]

PICTOR·ES

Heinricus Füllmaurer.

SCV

ERIS,

Albertus Meyer.

OR

OSA
Roſen.

As at Sissinghurst the roses are here under-planted with other things (such as pinks and *Saponaria ocymoides*) to extend the garden's season – it begins with polyanthus and aubretias – and to complement the roses themselves. Later interest is maintained by a long double herbaceous border, broken in the centre by a pool which bisects the whole garden.

An even newer garden with similar aims is now established at the other end of England, at Castle Howard near York. Again a walled kitchen garden is the site, hidden, as was the rule, from the eighteenth-century idealized landscape around the house. The classical façade of the gardener's house is the focus from which the design proceeds with yew hedges and architectural trellis frames to provide height. To these are trained the stronger forms.

Sissinghurst and Mottisfont derive their charm and effect from the 'cottage garden' tradition and the use of old roses. The conventional modern rose garden depends almost exclusively on those factors that make modern hybrid roses so popular: their brilliant colours, remontancy, floriferousness and regularity of growth combined with ease of cultivation. Such paragons, flowering from June to October inclusive, are obviously less in need of help from other plants to extend the season of interest in areas devoted to them. And hence, all over the temperate world, rose gardens flourish in sizes varying from the minute to the monolithic. The biggest are not always necessarily the best.

Only a tiny representative of the wealth of spectacular rose gardens that are to be seem can be considered here. European capital cities offer good material, and none more splendid that in Geneva, where roses have taken over whole areas of the city. For a mile along the Quai Gustave Ador, rose beds set in grass follow the edge of Lake Geneva. And these lead to the *roseraie* at the Parc de la Grange. The original plantings date respectively from 1936-1939 and 1945-1946.

Here is a highly formal rose garden, the beds being again set in grass and each holding one cultivar. Great care is taken with the colour arrangement of adjacent beds. The ground rises in three levels with a great pergola on top draped with climbing roses and wistarias and from here the full pattern of the garden is seen with its canals, fountains and sheets of colour provided by, if the *quai* and *roseraie* are combined, some 25,000 roses.

Moving west to Spain, roses are superbly represented at the Rosaleda del Parque del Oeste in Madrid. The basic ground plan is unusual, consisting of a large semi-circle. The arc of the semi-circle is described by a huge pergola covered with spectacular climbers and as the garden is entered by a flight of steps in the centre of the flat area; these enveloping arms of the pergola appear to enfold the whole. An axial walk leads to a fountain which is repeated by even bigger jets in the center of the pergola. These fall into a white marble basin over which a statuary group presides.

Each side of the main walk, further paths divide the ground into innumerable beds building up a vast parterre. Each bed holds about 100 bush and standard Hybrid Teas or Floribundas and the effect of the whole makes this one of the great rose gardens of Europe.

The first rose garden in Rome was planted between 1928 and 1931 on the ruins of Nero's Palace, the Domus Aurea, but the new Municipal Rose Gardens lie astride the Via di Valle Murcia on the slopes of the Aventino, one of Rome's seven hills. All around the natural amphitheatre of the garden are the typical Mediterranean cypresses, black and pointing, and, by comparison, the open umbrellas of stone pines. Gaps in the trees show the red ruins of the Palace of the Caesars beyond.

The garden contains more than 1,000 different roses, mainly modern, but older forms and species are represented as well. Again, as in Madrid, an unbroken, curving pergola around the crest of the amphitheatre crowns the garden and offers support to 200 different climbing roses.

All of these capital city rose gardens have annual competitions for new roses. In continental Europe the system employed is to grow bush roses for two years and climbers for three, after which periods the judging takes place. The varying climate of Europe makes it possible for judges and other keen rosarians to begin their competition year at the Via di Valle Murcia before moving on to the Rosaleda del Parque del Oeste, to Bagatelle and then to the Parc de la Grange.

In eastern Germany the rose garden of Sangerhausen, some forty miles north of Weimar, is remarkable in many ways. It preserves the biggest collection of nineteenth-century roses anywhere in the world. Varieties of Hybrid Perpetuals and early, pre-1914 Hybrid Teas run into hundreds. There are scores of Mosses and Gallicas, the original Bourbon rose is grown and even, it is said, Hume's Blush Tea-scented China still exists there. Clearly Sangerhausen has much to offer keen rosarians.

What also surprises western visitor is the informal way in which the roses are grown: there is not a billowing Sissinghurst informality but hard-pruned plants in series of beds without rigid plan. The site is a long, narrow oval rising from lakes at the lower end to rocky outcrops at the top, with the beds being fitted as thought best into the natural contours.

Informality of garden design does not in general associate well with the inevitable formality of modern roses conventionally pruned. And another example of this is in France. In 1964 the Roseraie at the Parc de la Tête d'Or was opened in Lyon. In its fourteen acres it has about 100,000 rose bushes, a remarkable sight – indeed it has been described as 'the finest rose-garden in Europe, if not in the whole world'. However, the associated meandering stream, the rustic bridges that cross it, the water-worn limestone which extends from poolside to rose bed all combine to build up an effect of restlessness. This, it seems, is not what rose gardens are about; and it comes as a relief to leave such contrived effects and walk away into the adjacent parkland around the lake.

Perhaps this attitude is both obscurantist and reactionary, but feelings of formal enclosure are such a part of the rose-garden ethic from the *Romaunt of the Rose* to the present day that it is difficult for those raised in that tradition not to accept it. Hence, there are obvious attractions of the small parterre-like rose garden in Glasgow's Pollock Park or the tree-surrounded rosary at Routh Park, Cardiff, which has a famous display of large and cluster-flowered roses, as well as climbers.

In London roses are best seen at the Queen Mary's Rose Garden in Regent's Park. For years the English Mecca for the dedicated rosarian was the Rose Society's garden at Bone Hill, on the edge of St Albans in Hertfordshire. The great advantage of these gardens was that in spite of their size, some twelve acres, there was still a domestic air.

In the centre was the Royal National Rose Society's headquarters, the modest turn-of-the-century house which provided a focus without the architectural pretensions that in so many gardens detract from the roses themselves. Although around 900 different species and cultivars were grown in the display garden alone, the overall effect impresses without daunting. Sadly, financial constraints have caused the house and half the land to be sold, but the Society is determined to rebuild its collection and continue to display new cultivars, the best of which move into the trade and out into our gardens.

One of the problems experienced by rose growers in more extreme continental climates is that of frost-hardiness. The origins of those ancestral roses which form the basis of modern-day roses lie mainly in the temperate or even the warm–temperate range. Hence a concern of many breeders, notably the Brownells in America and Kordes in Germany, has been to bring in other species which are evolutionarily adapted to extremes of temperature.

So successful has been this work that, throughout the two countries, fine rose gardens can be found, and one, Sangerhausen in Germany, has already been described. In Hartford, Connecticut, in spite of an equally fierce winter climate, the Elizabethan Park Rose Garden has been renowned for almost a century. Not only is it older than Bagatelle, Elizabeth Park has the oldest municipal rose garden in the world and rose trials have been held here since 1910.

The original garden, of approximately an acre in extent around a rustic summer house, contains a historic collection of Hybrid Perpetuals dating from 1903. Later plantings have doubled this area and now there are around 14,000 roses in over 1,000 forms – bushes, standards and climbers of various types, while some of the latter are conventionally grown on fences a particular feature has been made of pillar roses. This is a category frequently seen in catalogues but less often put into use. At Hartford seven-foot sitka spruce posts have dowelled laterals which provide a formalized tree ideal for rose growth.

From America's oldest rose garden to the biggest, it is necessary to travel 1,250 miles south-west to Tyler, Texas. Here are twenty-two acres of roses formally laid out and backed by fine woodland and enlivened with pools, fountains and gazebos. The beds are set in grass to help to 'cool' the flamboyance of 38,000 roses. Especially attractive is the sunken garden inside its high walls. Here roses are planted on several levels at the top of, and at the foot of, the retaining walls to provide a bank of flowers.

Although the peak period for flowering is mid-May, as befits so southern a site, the display is so well maintained that the annual Texas Rose Festival is not held until October, toward the very end of the season. The event of national attraction concentrates attention not only upon the municipal rose garden itself, but also upon the area around Tyler, which claims to grow half the world's commercial rose bushes. Over 20 million are sent out all over America each year.

While such rose gardens as Bone Hill, as the great municipal gardens of capital cities, or as Sissinghurst and Mottisfont are able to 'do the rose proud' on a considerable scale, these categories by no means exhaust the possibilities of where to view good roses. Every parks department in the temperate regions grows roses. It is estimated that in Britain eighty per cent of the private gardens grow roses (in the United States the figure is probably more like half that). Nor should the commercial growers be forgotten; not only do they provide the initial material for the rest of us, the displays in their fields and demonstration plantings around their buildings are often superb.

There is, however, a responsibility which all gardens share. Gertrude Jekyll put it with typical force nearly a century ago. There is: 'a duty we owe to our gardens … to a state of mind and artistic conscience that will not tolerate bad or careless combination or any misuse of plants … [it is by] thoughtful care and definite intention that they shall form a part of a harmonious whole.'

[1] Didymus Mountain, *The Gardener's Labyrinth*, 1560s

[2] John Harris, *Gardens of Delight: The Rococo English Landscape of Thomas Robins the Elder*, 1979

[3] Mark Laird, *The Flowering of the Landscape Garden*, 1999

[4] Russell Page, *The Education of a Gardener*, 1962

[5] V. Sackville-West, *Journal of the Royal Horticultural Society*, vol LXXVIII, 1953.

[6] Allen Paterson, *The Garden of Britain: Hampshire, Dorset and the Isle of Wight*, 1978.

The following pages show plates 9–11

CHAPTER 6

THE NINETEENTH CENTURY

The second main period in the development of garden roses as we know we them begins, conveniently, around 1800. We have seen the gradual development since early times in accidental fits and starts. The number of types of roses available increased as mutants were noticed and as new species were brought to Europe from all over the world. Until the late eighteenth century, however, with the sexuality of plants not being generally understood, hybridization occurred only by fortunate accident; and even when it was understood problems of sterility, incompatibility and polyploidy had still to be overcome. Understanding of the latter especially has come very late.

Most garden roses before 1800 were therefore of the interrelated group known as the *Gallicinae,* with *R. gallica* being a base-line from which the Damasks, Centifolias, Mosses and Albas had ultimately sprung. Interest, improved technology and further introductions now combined to provide the impetus for a great leap forward, to the production of roses which the eighteenth-century rosarians could hardly have imagined in their wildest flights of fancy.

The initial spur was the introduction, to a receptive gardening audience, of the China roses. Our western civilization, based upon Europe, is apt to forget, foolishly, that other cultures have earlier and no less sophisticated traditions of ornamental plant growing. This is the case, in particular, of China. Detailed treatises and recognizable depictions date from times at which Europe was still in the depth of the Dark Ages.

Screen paintings of 1,000 years ago show the delicate, slightly nodding flower and distinctive foliage of what became known, sensibly enough, as the China rose, *R. chinensis* (though, of course, there are many other distinct species from that country, any one of which could have appropriated the name had it got to Linnaeus first). Dr Hurst notes that in a painting by the Florentine artist, Agnolo Bronzino, dated 1529, a cascade of decidedly China roses is depicted, and he suggests that it is entirely possible that this rose got to Italy, perhaps by the land spice-route and thence to Venice, during the late Renaissance. That it did not spread far can be deduced, perhaps (as with *R. moschata*, another early oriental import), from its lack of frost-hardiness.

The first herbarium specimen in existence is dated 1733: of greater significance are those of Linnaeus in his collections which are held by the Linnean Society of London in Burlington House, Piccadilly. A Blush Tea-China, probably from Peter Osbeck's (a pupil of Linnaeus) Canton collections of 1751, is taken as the type. A China rose was in cultivation at the Chelsea Physic Garden in 1759, at the Princess Augusta's garden at Kew ten years later, and at the insatiable gardener, Dr Fothergill's, in Essex soon after. From England scions went south to the Continent.

Yet surprisingly, no use seems to have been made of these, and the subsequent significance of China roses fell to four separate introductions from 1792 to 1824.

These Dr Hurst refers to as the four Stud Chinas. The earliest is welcomed under the name of *R. semperflorens* by William Curtis in his *Botanical Magazine* dated December, 1794, in enthusiastic tones.

> We are induced to consider the rose here represented as one of the most desirable plants in point of ornament ever introduced; its flowers, large in proportion to the plant, are semi-double, and with great fragrance; they blossom during the whole of the year, more sparingly indeed in the winter months; the shoot itself is more hardy than most greenhouse plants, and will grow in so small a compass of earth, that it may be reared almost in a coffee cup … For this most invaluable acquisition, our country is indebted to the late Gilbert Slater Esq. whose untimely death every person must deplore…

This then is the Chinese Monthly rose which, with its relations introduced soon after, is in the parentage of almost all modern garden roses. In particular it became in Italy the parent of the Portland Rose and grandparent of the first Hybrid Perpetual.

To add to Slater's Crimson China, there soon appeared Parson's Pink China in 1793. This could have come to Sir Joseph Banks from the Macartney embassy to China which also introduced *R. bracteata* (see page 102). It was soon distributed in Britain whence it went to France and to America. Ease of propagation helped and, as Curtis remarks, it 'is kept without the least possible trouble and propagated without difficulty by cuttings and suckers'.

It soon proved to be highly fertile and Thory and Redouté (they were later to collaborate in producing the magnificent work *Les Roses*) were raising seedlings in Paris from it as early as 1798. Through the agency, it is presumed, of the brothers Louis and Philippe Noisette, who were nurserymen respectively in Paris and Charleston, South Carolina, it was used in Charleston by a wealthy rice planter, John Champneys, to produce with *R. moschata* the pink climber he called Champneys' Pink Cluster. An early mutant of Parson's rose was a miniature which is in the ancestry of our twentieth-century Poulsen Roses.

Slater's and Parson's China roses are still in cultivation and have been the subject of cytological study. The former has been shown to be triploid and the latter a simple diploid. The second pair of Stud Chinas, however, are probably no longer in existence. Hume's Blush Tea-Scented China was introduced in 1809 and, finally in the group, Park's Yellow Tea-Scented was brought from China in 1824 by one of the increasingly frequent plant-hunting expeditions sponsored by the Royal Horticultural Society. The colour of the latter made it highly desirable as the only source of good yellow in breeding programmes (the use of the old *R. foetida* did not come until later), and both became important in the development of Tea Roses.

The 'Tea' scent (rather like that of dried China tea) is really the property of the huge *R. gigantea* which throws out long trails of suitably enormous cream flowers in its native habitat of Upper Burma and Yunnan. The species was not collected until 1888 or 1889 (authorities differ) and is a plant only for the largest and warmest gardens. It flowers well, for example, on the French Riviera. But enquiries into the China roses show all but the first Stud China to be hybrids, grown for centuries in Chinese gardens, between the wild Crimson China and this, the wild Tea rose. Its accidental influence in the Old Stud Chinas and the continual hybridization to which they were subjected quickly produced a range of climbing tea-scented roses.

Seeds from Champneys' Pink Cluster were germinated by Philippe Noisette in Charleston and from the plants he selected and sent to his brother in Paris, one became known at the Blush Noisette or French Noisette rose. This is the original Noisette rose named formally by Redouté as *R. noisettiana*. Some of the earliest Noisettes are still grown, such as 'Aimée Vibert' raised at Angers in France in 1828. Ellen Willmott (*The Genus Rosa*, 1912) records that the raiser, J.-P. Vibert, wrote to the English nurseryman Lee 'to announce the magnificent new Rose he had raised and named after his daughter Aimée, he said that the English when they saw it would go down on their knees.' While there is no recorded instance of such genuflection it is interesting to note that Gertrude Jekyll in 1902, Ellen Willmott in 1914 ('It remains the most beautiful white Noisette we have') and Graham Thomas in 1978 ('it is, after all, the only perpetual flowering white rambler of any quality') think equally highly of this long-lived rose.

As soon as Park's Yellow China rose became available it was brought into the Noisette range and the production began of yellow tea-scented roses of both climbing and shrubby habit. Further breeding left Noisette characteristics behind and emphasized those of *R. gigantea* and the 1840s, 1850s and 1860s saw the appearance of such famous and exquisite roses as (in order of appearance) 'Céline Forestier,' 'Gloire de Dijon' and the green-gold 'Maréchal Niel'. All have superb scent but in England are sadly, even in the warmer parts, toward the northern limit of their success range. In the United States they need to be considered as zone nine plants.

The names of these roses emphasize the French influence, epitomized by the Empress Josephine and Redouté, on nineteenth-century rose breeding. While the Noisettes were developing, a further group of new roses appeared in parallel. On the former French colony of l'Île de Bourbon, now Réunion, roses were commonly used as hedges: two sorts especially, the old Autumn Damask and Parson's Pink China. A chance hybrid was found by the keeper of the Botanic Garden there, M Breon. Seeds of this intermediate rose were sent by Breon to Paris in 1819. They produced the first Bourbon roses with highly desirable characteristics: repeat flowering, rich colour, nearly evergreen foliage and delightful scent inherited from the Damask grandparent.

The best of the early Bourbon roses are still grown, such as the lovely soft pink 'Souvenir de la Malmaison' introduced in 1843; this fine bush is almost always in flower. 'Mme Pierre Oger' appeared in 1878 as a bud mutation from the earlier 'La Reine Victoria'. 'Mme Pierre' has delicate cup-shaped flowers which seem to reflect the weather. Mr Thomas described this (*Old Shrub Roses*, 1961): 'When first open on a cool day "Mme Pierre Oger" is of a soft, warm, creamy flesh, and in dull weather may remain so; in sunny weather the sun warms the petals or the portions of them that it touches to a clear rose, and in very hot weather a really intense colour develops.' This rose and its parent, he says, 'are unique period pieces' which accounts for so much of their appeal today.

As the century proceeds it becomes more and more difficult to maintain in any account a clear separation of these races of garden roses. Representatives from different groups were crossed, back crossed and crossed again. Though variously described as a Noisette or a Climbing Tea, 'Gloire de Dijon', for example, is the product of the Bourbon 'Souvenir de Malmaison' and an unnamed strong-growing Tea rose. It has, therefore, Tea-rose parentage from both sides which perhaps accounts for its scent and strange but lovely colouring – a suede-yellow with tinges of pink and apricot varying in strength, as in 'Mme Pierre Oger', according to the weather.

'Gloire de Dijon' also has *R. chinensis* blood to provide that continuity of flower which we now take for granted but which was, as will have been seen since earliest times, a sort of rosarian lodestone. (This ultimate desideratum, in combination with a search for unusual colours, led in some cases to the neglect of that essential quality of the rose – its scent.)

Continuity, or remontancy, of flower is a feature of another race of nineteenth-century roses, the Hybrid Perpetuals. The first of these as an acceptably distinct race appeared in the 1830s. The origins of the Perpetuals (or Remontants as they were known in France) go back to the famous Portland Rose and its direct derivative, the 'Rose du Roi' which Souchet raised at the garden of Louis XVIII at St Cloud in 1816. The Duchess of Portland, whose name is carried by a resultant small race of roses, had obtained a relatively remontant scarlet rose from Italy. It seems likely to have been a China-Damask-Gallica hybrid and was taken up by French breeders especially. Its early 'Rose du Roi' offspring was a considerable improvement – flowering more often and without the special pruning which the Portland Rose (and, it will be recalled, the classical autumn-flowering rose) needed.

Hybrids between the 'Rose du Roi' and the developing Hybrid China roses produced the race of plants which were larger flowered and more certainly all-summer through flowerers than the Portland: these Hybrid Perpetuals (or HPs) had not a fully satisfactory title because not all were as perpetual as was hoped. But hybrid they certainly were combining genes (and hence characteristics) from the old European garden roses and from new Chinas and Teas in a hitherto unprecedented way.

The great breeders of Hybrid Perpetuals were Sisley of Lyon and Laffay of Auteuil in France. The race of bush roses was vigorous and hardy with a colour range from white through the pinks and reds to deep plum-purple, and they dominated with the Teas the garden rose scene for almost the rest of the century. Early named Hybrid Perpetuals were 'Mme Laffay' and 'Duchess of Sutherland' and 1842 saw what Dr Hurst describes as 'that famous "Rose de la Reine" with its large, strangely cupped flowers of a beautiful lilac-rose and fragrant as a Cabbage rose.'

Later cultivars within the Hybrid Perpetual group varied greatly in their amount of scent and in their habit of autumn flowering, as well as in the more obvious differences of size and colour. One of the loveliest, and still in cultivation, is 'Général Jacqueminot' of 1852. This has Bourbon blood and is a strong crimson-scarlet with a penetrating Damask scent – a characteristic passed on to numbers of its descendants.

At this mid-century point, while old gardens still maintained stocks of the traditional Damasks, Centifolias and Gallicas, interest was concentrated upon the two parallel groups of Teas and Hybrid Perpetuals. This was no doubt inevitable, especially with the social attitudes of the time having moved from eighteenth-century aristocratic elegance to more bourgeois ideals in which outward show took a prime part, and for a much greater proportion of the population. Doubtless too from this time, as the flood of new roses became available, unfashionable types, many of great historic value, were lost for good.

The next goal of rose breeders was to combine the hardiness and vigour of the Hybrid Perpetuals with the elegance, range of colours and scent of the Tea roses. The highly regarded 'La France' which the French grower Guillot produced in 1867 was one of the first, but some time elapsed before the group was sufficiently distinct to be recognized. In 1884 they were officially called Hybrid Teas. Without these, our modern rose gardens would not be the places they are.

Breeders found great difficulty at first in using the early Hybrid Teas (as retrospectively we can call them). This has been shown[1] to be because, as with the early Chinas and Bourbons, 'La France' was a triploid, and hence effective chromosomal pairings with diploids and tetraploids were unlikely. However, after years of apparent failure, varieties were bred which had reached the tetraploid chromosome number and there was suddenly almost an explosion of new garden HTs. And, as the nineteenth century drew to a close, this was the group which displaced all but the best of the Hybrid Perpetuals.

But, as always, it seemed that the new race lacked something – a clear strong yellow. To another great rose breeder of Lyon, Pernet-Ducher, the answer was obvious – to use the clear strong colour of the Austrian Yellow, *R. foetida*. And for five years, from 1883 to 1888, he crossed literally thousands of Hybrid Perpetual flowers from many varieties with the Persian Yellow, the Austrian's double variant, before he obtained his first success. Using 'Antoine Ducher' as the female parent, at last a few seeds were gathered and of these only two germinated. The difficulty was that *R. foetida*, although given specific status, is almost certainly an ancient hybrid and after a thousand years of cultivation had become virtually sterile.

One of the two new roses flowered in 1891, but tragically it proved to be sterile. The other flowered two years later and appeared undistinguished but, of course, possessed the coveted genetic colouring potential of the

Austrian Yellow. The unnamed seedling was crossed with various Hybrid Teas and eventually produced the first really yellow Hybrid Tea. Suitably named 'Soleil d'Or,' this first Pernet rose was exhibited at Lyon in 1878 and heralded the brilliant Hybrid Teas of the present century. *R. foetida* and *R. foetida bicolor* brought this brilliance into the rose garden. Their contribution was not, however, an unmixed blessing. In the hands of rose growers without much colour sense (and some seem to have none) the rose garden scene can now show such a kaleidoscope of colours as to half-blind the sensitive: worse, these two species introduced a lack of fragrance and susceptibility to black-spot disease so as to, in the opinion of some, entirely negate their virtues. Such disadvantages have been extremely difficult to overcome, though such success as there has been will be discussed in the next chapter.

This emphasis upon the development of Hybrid Perpetuals and Hybrid Teas is inevitable in any historical account of roses, especially because to many people these are 'real' roses. Certainly they are the most seen. There are, however, other races of roses which, although less spectacular, are still of importance in the garden scene and some have a nineteenth-century origin.

While some of the groups or races of roses described in this chapter continued to be used and went on to join with yet more, others developed their own small but nevertheless distinctive world – like a tribe of men hemmed in by mountains – unaffected by and unaffecting the moving world outside. Such are the Scots or Burnet roses, forms and later hybrids of *R. spinosissima.* The Latin superlative is well earned as the numerous straight sharp prickles are intermixed with stiff bristly hairs so that the stems are hidden within this protective enclosure.

The species has an enormous natural distribution. Growing in sandy soils, especially near the sea, in Europe it may be found wild from Iceland to Norway southward to Spain, Italy and Macedonia, and in Asia from Central Russia and the Caucasus to Manchuria and north-west China, southward to Asia Minor. Always it is a low twiggy bush, running about and pushing up suckers to form almost impenetrable thickets.

In spite of its frequency, however, it seems not to have brought into cultivation early. Perhaps it had no reputation in the 'virtues' so essential to the early herbalists. Gerard fails to mention it, nor does Johnson in his extended second edition of Gerard of 1633. But seven years later John Parkinson's *Theatrum botanicum* has a clear description and an illustrative woodcut under the names in Latin and English of '*Rosa pimpinellifolia sive Pomifera minor* – the small Burnet Rose.' The leaves are, says Parkinson,

> seeming like unto a Burnet leafe for the forme and number set together: the flowers are single small and white without any sent *(sic)*, after which come small round heads but black when they are ripe full of seede as in other roses.

The Burnet referred to in the seventeenth century, as now, is *Poterium sanguisorba*, a little rosaceous plant of the chalklands (whose pinnate leaves are ideal for adding interest to sandwiches, as they taste of cucumber).

Miller is terse about the plant, though he does say that it has an agreeably musky scent. (In fact the double white has a distinctly lily-of-the-valley perfume.) So it comes as a sudden surprise to read the description taken from a paper given before the Horticultural Society of London in 1820 of how this little rose was suddenly taken up, like a waif from the streets, and plunged into society. The Professor Higgins to the Eliza Doolittle of the Burnet rose was Robert Brown of Perth who, with his brother,

> transplanted some of the wild Scotch Roses from the Hill of Kinnoul, in the neighbourhood of Perth, into their nursery-garden: one of these bore flowers slightly tinged with red, from which a plant was raised, whose flowers exhibited a monstrosity appearing as if one or two flowers came from the bud, which was a little tinged with red: these produced seed, from whence some semi-double flowering plants were obtained …

In less than a couple of decades double varieties were listed in a range of colours from the original white through yellow, blush and red to bicoloured forms. Well before the mid-century, Miss Willmott asserts, British nurserymen were offering between two and three hundred 'Scotch Roses.' It is, however, extremely likely that, because they vary so much and so easily from seed, their number was inflated by a large amount of synonymy.

These little roses seem not to have appealed greatly to the European rosarians but to northern gardeners this accommodating and ineradicably hardy race of charming roses was of considerable value.

Robert Brown of Perth is also given the credit by Ellen Willmott (following Simon and Cochet, 1899) for raising 'Stanwell Perpetual', a delightful spinosissima hybrid which is still of great garden value. Thomas Rivers, however, asserts that 'The Stanwell Perpetual I believe was raised from seed in Mr Lee's nursery at Stanwel,' which is in Middlesex.

Twice as tall as the usual Burnet roses and flowering later, Miss Jekyll considered Stanwell's Perpetual's rather lax habit its only drawback and recommended (*Roses for English Gardens,* 1902) that three should be planted together a foot apart to help hold each other up. While Stanwell Perpetual is still available for keen growers and, as is obvious, is well worth growing, the number of Burnet roses has declined dramatically; fewer are now available than after Robert Brown's first selection. This is a pity. Their special use is discussed in the next chapter.

Another small group of roses has a Scottish origin, though one which is very confusing. These are the Ayrshire roses. Samuel Curtis (having taken over the

Botanical Magazine at the death of his brother William) published on 1st March, 1819, a figure and description of *Rosa arvensis*, 'The Ayrshire Rose'. Curtis says he cannot find anything about this plant which differs markedly from the ordinary wild white *R. arvensis* (the Musk rose of Shakespeare, see page 234). And indeed that is the plant which was drawn for him.

> It has been known some years in our nurseries, under the name of the Ayrshire Rose, but upon what grounds it has been so called is difficult to say, for upon the strictest enquiry as we are informed by Sir Joseph Banks, no rose of the kind could be heard of there or in any part of Scotland.

This appears, however, to have been a nonsense even when it was written. Banks himself was supplied with the true white rambling Ayrishire rose in 1811 and several references to it predate the *Botanical Magazine* account.

It seems that seeds of *R. arvensis* were germinated at Loudoun Castle in Ayrshire, having come, ostensibly, from Canada. But as neither that species, nor *R. sempervirens* (with which the Ayrshires have been thought to show some affinity) are native to North American, it must be assumed they are of garden origin.

Their value in the early decades of the last century was emphasized because of the dearth of other good, really hardy climbing roses. They could be trained on extensive walls, allowed to scramble up trees and into hedgerows (and this informal use clearly occurred some years before Robinsonian eulogies of naturalistic use of plants).

Miss Jekyll lumps a couple of Ayrshire roses such as 'Dundee Rambler' and 'Bennett's Seedling' with definite offspring of *R. sempervirens* including 'Félicité et Perpétue' and 'Flora' with certain others under the sensible title of Climbing Cluster roses. While the former groups are almost completely superseded now, Miss Jekyll's championing of 'Garland' (a *multiflora* x *moschata* cross) is so convincing as to encourage any insomniac gardener to grow it.

> It is well worth getting up at 4 a.m. on a mid-June morning to see the tender loveliness of the newly opening buds; for, beautiful though they are at noon, they are better still when just awakening after the refreshing influence of the short summer night.

The *R. sempervirens* hybrids were the product of M Jacques' work at Château Neuilly in France in the 1820s and early 1830s. Jacques' lovely 'Félicité et Perpétue' of 1827 is still available and as valuable as ever with its robust constitution, near evergreen foliage and great clusters of tight double pale-cream flowers.

Another little French group which appeared at about this time are the Boursault roses. They have an unusual parentage in that with *R. chinensis* they bring in another species, possibly the thornless *R. blanda*, the alpine *R. pendulina*, otherwise virtually unused by hybridists. The original raiser is not known, although there are several attributions, and they carry the name of M Boursault who, around 1800, had a noteworthy garden and collection of roses in Paris. It could actually have occurred there or its owner may have been just a dedicatee. A number of forms developed, such as 'Old Red Boursault', 'Inermis', 'Amadis' and 'Mme de Sancy de Parabère' (these last three have inherited the thornless character of *R. pendulina*). But sadly all are virtually scentless and apt to produce irregular flowers.

It was logical that American breeders should use their native pink July-flowering Prairie rose, *R. setigera*, to produce hardy climbing roses. The species is found wild from Florida and Texas in the south to as far north as the Great Lakes. But although the earliest varieties, such as Samuel Feast's 'Baltimore Belle' of the 1830s, had great initial popularity, they were soon replaced by cultivars reflecting the oriental *synstylae* (see Appendix) species which were introduced during the mid-century.

Of these, *R. multiflora* has had some effect upon garden roses of several types. The true species (also known, erroneously, as *R. polyantha*) was introduced, like some other orientals, only after garden forms of it had reached the West. Some of these are variously described and referred to in the available texts. In Redouté (*Roses,* vol II,

1821) it is mentioned that William Anderson, who had been appointed curator of the Chelsea Physic Garden in 1814, gave a single-flowered multiflora to Louis Noisette, whose Paris nursery was soon offering it for sale. Other than this, however, it seems that the normally available forms of this species were the Chinese garden cultivars with double red or pink flowers. One of these was known as the 'Seven Sisters Rose' (once given specific status as *R. platyphylla*). Another was the initially very popular 'Crimson Rambler', now quite superseded by later introductions. Miss Jekyll, who had in fullest measure that 'poetic feeling and the painter's eye' which the great gardeners possess, is gently damning:

> Those of us whose eyes are trained to niceties of colour-discrimination wish that the tint of this fine flower had been just a shade different … if it had just a little of that rank quality that it possesses slightly in excess, it would have been a still more precious thing in our garden.[2]

The definitely wild plant introduced in 1862, if only for the biggest gardens, can be a much finer plant with long loose panicles each made up of a couple of hundred small white bramble-like flowers. There is a clear and delicate scent. Alfred Parsons' lovely plate of it in *The Genus Rosa* is perhaps over-kind: noteworthy, however, is his careful delineation of the fringed stipules typical to this species and its offspring.

No doubt many people have grown this rose by something of a mistake. It was commonly used as an understock for garden cultivars (it roots easily from cuttings and a thornless form is available). If the chosen rose dies, very often the stock puts up strong shoots and in a year or two makes a fine flowering plant – though it is not one for the conventional rose beds in which it may appear.

While the multiflora climbers had a relatively short reign, being replaced by derivatives of *R. wichuraiana* (see below), the species contributed to a very different group of roses. This was begun by Guillot, that noted rose breeder from Lyon, in whose nursery the wild white multiflora fortuitously crossed with the Dwarf Pink China. Great diversity emerged from the first seeds collected but significance revealed itself in the second generation when two of the seedlings were seen to be dwarf. There was little doubt as to their parentage and they were given the cultivar names of 'Paquerette' (pure white) and 'Mignonette' (pink and white): both grew only seven inches or so in height and were clearly a genetic breakthrough.

The general name for this group has seen some vicissitudes. Dwarf Polyantha was the name for a long time, but it seems best to maintain the title Pompon as Gertrude Jekyll recommended in 1902 or Polypoms as they are now generally called. Most of the important derivatives of this class did not come until our own century, but the Tea Rose influence was brought in with two exquisite French cultivars of the 1880s. Dureuil's 'Perle d'Or' is soft buff-yellow and Ducher's 'Cécile Brunner' fresh pink. Both have perfectly formed miniature Tea rose flowers on dainty low bushes. In 1894 a plant of the latter in California produced a climbing sport known as 'Climbing Cécile Brunner'. The flowers are as perfect as on the type but carried in profusion on a plant that may attain twenty feet in height; this is one of the loveliest of garden roses in any group, but sadly not remontant.

While the British flora contains over a dozen wild rose species, of which two or three have made minimal contributions to the development of the garden rose, only one has been generally accepted in its own right as a plant fit to be brought into gardens. This is the famous Eglantine (*R. eglanteria*) or Sweetbrier. In the wild it is an early colonizer of ungrazed chalkland pasture and has a wide European and Asiatic distribution from Spain in the west to North India in the east. Everywhere it is renowned for the fragrance that the whole plant throws upon the air after a shower of rain. Not surprisingly therefore, there are old selected sports or seedlings such as the doubles 'Manning's Blush' and 'La Belle Distinguée', but it was left until the end of the nineteenth century for a wider range to be developed. This was done in England by Lord Penzance in the 1890s. These Penzance Briers are *R. elganteria* (especially in 'Janet's Pride' form, (see page 79) crossed with various species and Hybrid Perpetuals to produce strong ten-feet high shrubs with brightly coloured flowers and often a good autumn display of fruit as well. The essential sweetbrier apple-like fragrance has, of course, been carefully retained. Named cultivars commemorate the raiser, Lord Penzance and Lady Penzance (suede yellow and copper-coloured respectively). The lovely hue of these comes from *R. foetida bicolor* and the Persian Yellow; so too does the susceptibility to black spot

'Meg Merrilees' is a bright rosy-crimson and without the 'Austrian' blood is a better plant.

Of Lord Penzance, Miss Jekyll wrote:

> It seems as though this eminent lawyer, who is some of the years of his mature practice had to put the law in effect decreeing the separation of unhappy human couples, had sought mental refreshment in the leisure of his latest days by devoting it to the happy marriages of Roses. Though his name will ever stand high in the records of legal practice, it is doubtful whether in years to come it will not be even more widely known in connection with the Roses he has left us, the fruits of the recreation of his last years of failing strength.

Miss Jekyll has been proved right – who now remembers Lord Penzance the lawyer?

The date of introduction of the Japanese Ramanas rose, *R. rugosa*, is ascribed to Lee and Kennedy, the

Kensington nurserymen, as far back as 1796 (Willmott) or 1845 by the Royal Horticultural Society's *Dictionary of Gardening*. It is another seaside rose – a Japanese Burnet, it might be said – and demonstrates the tightness of growth evolved for succeeding in such a habitat. The species is a clear red, heavily fragrant, above strong foliage and is followed by huge hips which are highly decorative in their own right. Among early hybrids with clear Rugosa parentage is 'Blanc Double de Coubert' which Cochet-Cochet brought out in 1892. Just ten years later Miss Jekyll describes it as the 'whitest Rose of any known' and its air of strong wellbeing combined with a positively ambrosial scent makes it still widely loved and grown. The same firm produced the exquisite 'Roseraie de l'Hay' in 1901. Unfortunately these diploid Rugosas proved to be highly sterile and seemed to have reached a dead end. However, movement forward has now become possible.

It would have been convenient to follow *R. multiflora* as a source of valuable climbing roses with the species which can be seen as its even more productive successor – *R. wichuraiana*. But as its effects so strongly move the story into the twentieth century it is better to deal with it now, at the end of this chapter.

Rosa wichuraiana is now known to be native to Taiwan, Eastern China and to Korea; it was first collected and introduced, however, from Japan in 1891. It has fine heads of creamy white flowers whose rather reflexed petals set off each great boss of yellow stamens. They open in late summer and have a strong, sweet scent. What is particularly noticeable is that this rose is a natural ground-coverer, rooting as it goes and developing a splendid evergreen carpet. It is interesting to read Miss Jekyll's enthusiasm for this rose, only ten years after its introduction (which says much for the spread of nineteenth-century propagation and distribution).

She remarks, too, that already useful hybrids were being produced from it. The year 1900 saw the introduction in France of the fine old 'Alberic Barbier' whose creamy yellow buds and ivory open flowers have happily been a part of so many garden scenes for over a century.

In America, a year later, came the pink rambler 'Dorothy Perkins'. This is such a traditional cottage garden plant as to give the impression that it is of far older origin; even brighter is 'American Pillar' (1902), one of the early Van Fleet hybrids, in which Dr Walter Van Fleet used the Prairie Rose and some Hybrid Perpetual blood.

As the new century gathered momentum, so did some of the emphasis of rose breeding move across the Atlantic, with Van Fleet, Horvath and Walsh. In France, however, from 1890 work was done on the huge but tender *R. gigantea*, which, it will be recalled, provided the 'tea' scent via three of the Stud Chinas to so many later roses. Hitherto such importance had been placed upon frost-hardiness for cold climates that the requirements of warmer ones had been given little thought by rose

یا غیاث المستغیثین رحمتی

breeders. This is an area to which the Australian, Alister Clark, has been devoting increased attention. It moves forward in parallel with the use of further species and the reworking of old ones in different combinations.

[1] Ann Wylie, 'The History of Garden Roses,' *Royal Horticultural Society Journal*, 1954.

[2] Gertrude Jekyll, *Roses for English Gardens,* 1902

Chapter 7

Roses of the Twentieth Century

At the turn of the century on both sides of the Atlantic, rose-growing was obviously poised to develop at an unprecedented rate. Highly influential gardening writers – often, like William Robinson and Gertrude Jekyll, very effective practitioners as well – eulogized the diversity and potential of the rose. A prosperous middle class in the apparent security of a pre-World War era took to gardening as never before in the expanding fashionable suburbs of all large towns. The diversity of roses available seemed never-ending. Yet such was the rate of new hybrids being distributed that, like fashion in clothes, varieties were discarded almost before they had time to show their potential.

The following passage from Robertson's monthly publication *Flora and Sylva* (vol. iii, January 1905) demonstrates this. Like the shades of the notable people they were named after, most of these roses have disappeared 'as if they had never been'. Here is George H. Ellwanger with 'Rose Notes from Western New York':

> … Madame Jules Grolez has proved most satisfactory as a brilliant and showy Rose. Hélène Cambier too has been exquisite throughout the season, and what a fragrance she disburses, similar to Malmaison, Madame Wagram, Comtesse de Turenne and Reine Nathalie de Serbie, Frau Geheimrath von Boch has a lovely complexion, but no physique. The new hybrid-tea Königen Carola, is a wonder the size of its rich rose blooms. Madame Jean Dupuy promises better than Frauziska Krüger. Friedrich Harms and Prince de Bulgarie are superb, and so are Prince Theodore Galitzine, Princess Beatrix, Madame Derepas-Matrat, and numerous others among the golden and orange beauties not forgetting Alliance France-Russe, Mdlle Jeanne Philippe and Mdlle Pauline Bersez … Madame Ravar, as you say, is a charmer worth knowing, though with her away one could pass the time right merrily with Hofgardendirektor Gralbener, and scarcely know the difference …

And so on for a couple of columns of truly dreadful horticultural name-dropping. If the source were not impeccable one would suspect an elaborate hoax.

Just as fifty years earlier the Hybrid Perpetuals had displaced the supremacy of the Damasks, Centifolias and

Gallicas, so now they in turn began to be ousted by the floods of new Hybrid Teas. Where they were once listed by the thousand, they have now even lost their separate classification and are, by some authorities, lumped in with their rivals.

It is fitting then that 1900 saw the introduction of Pernet-Ducher's epoch-making 'Soleil d'Or', the first near-golden Hybrid Tea rose. 'Rayon d'Or' ten years later became the first true yellow Hybrid Tea. These brought, as has already been remarked, not just the colour of the Austrian Yellow but its scentlessness and susceptibility to black spot disease. Lack of scent, however, cannot be blamed entirely upon *R foetida*. Pernet-Ducher's famous Hybrid Perpetuals 'Mme Caroline Testout,' dating from 1870 and still grown, has very little to offer in that respect.

Of the early Hybrid Teas very few indeed have kept their place in the lists, yet, as with any art form, the best is apt to maintain itself while lesser things perish. This is not to say that some cultivars lost to cultivation are not to be regretted – each, after all, is a unique combination of genes which can never be recreated and might have subsequent breeding potential. Yet it is unrealistic to expect the new not to elbow out the old.

Still with us is 'Ophelia,' which William Paul introduced as long ago as 1912. The classically shaped flowers are of pale pink, with each petal having a soft yellow base; it has also been a splendid parent of over two hundred different named roses and many fine derivatives still have its distinctive scent. 'Ophelia's' sport, 'Mme Butterfly' (Puccini's popular work was first produced in 1904) appeared soon after, adding a suffusion of apricot to the pink of its parent, and this too maintains its adherents in our gardens.

By the 1920s, some of today's famous families of rose breeders (and the calling does seem to engender great family solidarity, necessary no doubt because of the long-term nature of the work) were putting out new roses. The best are still with us. 'Shot Silk' came from Dickson's in 1924, and lives up to its name with its combination of carmine and buff-salmon shades.

The name of a compatriot nursery is maintained by our continuing to grow such fine roses as 'Mrs Sam McGredy' and 'McGredy's Yellow'. The first was introduced in 1929 and is remarkable for the complementary effect of its coppery foliage on the flowers which seem to pick up the same colour. The second, a lovely creamy yellow, appeared in 1933. Both have an earlier cultivar, 'The Queen Alexandra Rose' (probably now lost) in their parentage.

With the exception of one small departure from the norm in Rhode Island which began in the 1920s, this great class of Hybrid Tea roses is the product, almost entirely, of interbreeding within itself. Dr and Mrs Brownell, therefore, deserve credit for concentrating on the production of roses which combine the desirable flower size, shape and colour of conventional Hybrid Teas with the extreme frost-hardiness so necessary for the north-eastern United States and eastern Canada.

Using three of the turn-of-the-century Van Fleet hybrid *wichuraiana* Climbers, crossed with the splendid old HP 'Général Jacqueminot' and various Hybrid Teas, including 'Crimson Glory,' a valuable group of Hybrid Teas and Floribundas was developed which will accept low temperatures with impunity. They also have the enviable resistance to black spot inherited from the glossy leaved *R. wichuraiana.*

In Europe and Britain interest continued in widening the colour range to the truly remarkable extent which we enjoy today. Flowers may be self-coloured or suffused with other shades; inheritance from *R. foetida bicolor* may provide petals with different colours on the face and reverse of the petals. Of this type are Meilland's 'Sultane' (1946) and the even brighter 'Tzigane' (1951): both have a scarlet with yellow reverse colouration.

The flamboyance of many modern garden roses has led to something of a reaction against those cultivars which, in the proud words of one American rose catalogue, are 'bursting with flashy color' and current breeding emphasis is moving toward cultivational aspects, although no doubt there will still be a search for the fabled blue rose. (Tantau's 'Blue Moon' of 1964 is still the best in this line.)

Colour being gene-controlled, though in a complicated way that is still not fully understood, it may be that, although the potential of existing rose colours has been used is apparently every possible combination, gene mutation could still produce more. The way has already been demonstrated. In roses it has been shown that the anthocyanidin pigment cyanidin produces the scarlets and pinks while flavonal is responsible for the creams and yellows. But in the 1930s a pigment hitherto unknown to roses appeared giving the 'day-glow' brightness of the bright bedding 'geraniums.' This is known aptly as 'pelargonidin'; Tantau's 'Super Star', first distributed as 'Tropicana' – a clear luminous vermilion – is a fine example: a beautiful rose but difficult to use well in the garden.

Fortunately scent, that expected heirloom of roses, has been well considered in recent Hybrid Tea breeding. Not surprisingly the bicolours have little, but among the pinks 'Prima Ballerina' (Tantau, 1957) and red 'Papa Meilland' (Meilland, 1963) are outstanding.

So, too, is the delicious intoxicating fruitiness of 'Fragrant Cloud' (Tantau, 1963). That great rosarian, Harry Wheatcroft, described it as 'the most outstanding rose of all time,' though perhaps most people would award that palm to the famous 'Peace' (see page 253).

When it is remembered that *R. gigantea* is an ancestral parent of all Hybrid Tea roses, we should not be surprised that many cultivars have produced climbing sports. Looking at the lists, it is seen that about a decade usually elapses between the introduction of the bush type and that of the mutant. Many of these climbers are invaluable for garden decoration, although they are apt to be less free in their flowering then their precursors. Interestingly, the character of weak flower-stalks leading to nodding flowers, while undesirable in a bush rose, is ideal in a climber viewed, as it usually must be, from below: Kordes' lovely 'Climbing Crimson Glory' of 1946 is an excellent example.

Our usual expectation of a Hybrid Tea rose is of a perfectly shaped bloom on a long stem supported by just one or two buds. Yet many of the latest cultivars – 'Fragrant Cloud' is a good example – send up shoots with great heads of flowers, albeit each may be of Hybrid Tea size. Similarly, the class of garden roses which has been developed in this century in parallel, now called Floribundas, can frequently produce flowers of Hybrid Tea class. While there are still representatives of each group that are very distinct, there is a penumbral middle range in which they clearly overlap.

It is necessary to return to the beginning of the century to trace the development of these fine garden roses. It will be recalled that in the 1870s two derivatives of the Dwarf Pink China, 'Paquerette', and 'Mignonette', began a race known as Polypoms (Dr Hurst's coinage) or Dwarf Polyanthas. Those still seen are little bushes with tight heads of very double flowers and, although sadly scentless, they still have their uses in combination with herbaceous plants in a border where colour and continuity are the requirements. The lack of fragrance seems to have come in

The following pages show plates 12–14

1903 when the 'cottage-garden' 'Crimson Rambler' became a parent, and then in 1911 'Dorothy Perkins' was used in the development of further forms. Over two hundred and fifty named Polypoms existed at the height of their popularity. Many were consciously produced hybrids – selections from the huge number of seedlings actually raised – but over half have been shown to have been sports. 'Orléans Rose' was particularly unstable, with twenty-nine sports occurring on it.

While 'Cécile Brunner' (see page 165) was the first Tea Polypom right back in 1881, and hence began a delightful but small group of roses that have already been mentioned, little further work seems to have been done on this line. But in the 1920s the Danish firm of Poulsen produced a sensational group of bedding roses by bringing in Hybrid Tea blood. The Polypom 'Orléans Rose' of 1909 was crossed with the old single Hybrid Tea 'Red Star'. Two seedlings from this cross were named 'Else Poulsen' and 'Kirsten Poulsen' and were the first in a whole line of roses which proudly commemorate almost every member of that now famous family.

As, in the 1930s, Hybrid Tea blood was brought into a new Polypom cultivars, both the colour range and the type of flower shape became more varied. The name of the group moved to that of Hybrid Polyantha. Not many of the old Polypoms are still in cultivation and available from nurserymen 'The Fairy' (1932), rather like a low billowing *wichuraiana* rambler when planted en masse, is one such. But clearly, their role has not been entirely filled because De Ruiters brought out in the 1950s several new little roses of this type. They were suitably named, from the size point of view, after Snow White's seven dwarfs; otherwise not.

The modern group of roses which are predominant for spectacular massed display have this background. Known now as Floribundas, there are probably more new cultivars of this type produced annually than of all the rest of the roses put together. The pressure brought about by the constant stream of introductions is indicated in the fact that only perhaps the original multi-coloured 'Masquerade' (1949) and the lovely deep-crimson 'Frensham' of 1946 remain of their decade. Unfortunately but inevitably, continuous vegetative propagation is apt to result in a decline in vigour or increased susceptibility to disease, in 'Frensham's' case (and in that of 'Super Star') to rose powdery mildew.

From the 1950s we still have De Ruiter's charming 'Rosemary Rose' with reddish foliage of China rose type and flowers of almost Centifolia flatness: this has the fine old Bourbon type 'Grüss an Teplitz' as one parent. The enormously tall 'Queen Elizabeth' rose dates from 1956 and is still often seen.

While the brilliant flame and scarlet colours continued in a flood, certain breeders tended to concentrate upon softer, less blatant shades. Le Grice, in France, is one such, having produced 'Lilac Charm' in

1962 and the rich lilac-mauve 'Ripples' nine years later. Kordes' deservedly popular 'Iceberg' with its showers of blossom above delicate foliage also deserves mention as a hybrid (this is 'Robin Hood' x 'Virgo') which stands out immediately from the crowd.

While it is probably inevitable that the majority of garden rose breeding will continue to concentrate upon these two groups, the Hybrid Teas and the Floribundas, between which it becomes less and less easy to differentiate, twenty-first-century rose-growing has plenty more to offer and in many diverse forms. With the E. H. Wilson introductions of wild Chinese roses, large gardens particularly have been able to show the charm and potential in both flowers and fruit of unhybridized species. And certain breeders, sometimes at a virtually amateur (in the best sense of that word) level, have produced roses for special purposes by using parents which the big firms might consider unproductive.

One small yet important group which might come into that category is known as the Hybrid Musks. Crossed with the early Stud Chinas, it will be recalled, the true *R. moschata* is a part of the Autumn Damask (and hence the Bourbons) and of the Noisette roses. It is the use of this latter groupof roses (not the Musk rose itself) by firstly Peter Lambert in Germany between 1896 and 1920 and concurrently and then later by the Reverend Joseph Pemberton in Essex, England, which is of significance.

Of Lambert's Pillar roses twenty-five have been traced, in which he tried to breed frost-hardier roses of Noisette character by crossing Noisettes such as 'Rêve d'Or' with Teas, Polypoms and even with the 'Austrian Copper'. 'Aglaia' and 'Trier' were his first important introductions, the latter especially so as it became the parent of further 'Lambertianas' and also of some of Pemberton's Hybrid Musks, which are now by far the more highly regarded. These have, to some extent, found their true niche half a century after their introduction as mixed shrub border or high, loose hedging plants.

Pemberton used predominantly Hybrid Teas in his crosses with 'Trier' and its derivatives. One of the earliest still grown is 'Moonlight,' which came out in 1913. This has splendid sprays of cream-fading-to-white flowers, deliciously musk-rose scented, right through the season. Better known, and having 'Ophelia' as a parent, is 'Penelope,' with creamy-pink flowers. Most of Reverend Pemberton's rose introductions are triploid and hence they offered little hope to any hybridist who wished to take the group further. But one Hybrid Musk of 'Trier' blood with a Polypom is a diploid. This is 'Robin Hood'.

The German breeder Kordes picked 'Robin Hood' up for its frost-hardiness and crossing it with the Hybrid Tea 'J. C. Thornton' produced, surprisingly, two tetrapolid offspring. These two are 'Eva' of 1933 and 'Wilhelm' of the following year. This fortunate phenomenon made chromosomal pairing possible and hence they are in the parentage of large numbers of recent roses. 'Wilhelm', known as 'Skyrocket' in the United States, is highly praised by Graham Thomas, who finds that the blueness in the deep crimson (not far from 'Crimson Glory' in colour) makes it:

> one of the comparatively new shrub roses which can be used as a meeting point between the old roses and the moderns. As a shrub it leaves nothing to be desired; stalwart, bushy with few thorns on the great green shoots and handsome dark green leaves in plenty.[1]

Ironically, sister 'Eva' has been in the parentage of later roses which possess that dangerously brilliant mutant pigment cyanidin and which need such care in the choice of their neighbours in the garden. They include Boerner's 'Fashion' from America (1947), an oddly attractive and highly scented salmon-orange, if only it can be contained, and the vivid orange-scarlet 'Independence' (1950). This latter was originally named 'Sondermeldung' by the raiser Wilhelm Kordes, and may be so referred to in some texts. Further work with roses of Hybrid Musk origin continues by bringing in Floribunda and Hybrid Tea blood: all of this combines to make the distinction between some of the classes of roses more and more diffuse. The apricot 'Grandmaster' is one example here but it also demonstrates the likelihood of a loss of fragrance if the scented ancestry is too highly adulterated.

Where it can be said, on the one hand, that the speed of late twentieth-century rose breeding was like that of a river in spate which apparently sweeps all before it, there are, on the other hand, little back eddies which maintain themselves quietly until some alteration of the main current plucks them out for the world to see.

Robert Brown's early nineteenth-century Scots Burnet selections from the Hill of Kinnoul (see page 158), while appreciated at home, made little if any impact in Europe. Yet over 100 years later, when frost-hardiness was considered there to be of greater moment, the German firm of Kordes turned to *R. spinosissima* for its characteristic robustness. What has emerged is the 'Frühlings' group of early flowering shrub roses.

Several have the old American Hybrid Tea 'Joanna Hill' as a parent. In any consideration of twentieth-century roses this name comes up again and again. Descended from 'Ophelia' on both sides, 'Joanna Hill' is responsible for the vigour here and in many more conventional hybrids such as the famous 'Peace' (see page 253).

'Frühlingsgold' was the first use of the new Burnet group to be distributed, in 1937, and *R. spinosissima hispida* is the other parent. It makes a great six-foot-high bush, and as much across, with long arching sprays of intensely fragrant flowers. *R. spinosissima altaica* is the other half of 'Frühlingsduft,' a double pink-flushed creamy-white which Kordes brought out in 1949 and

'Frühlingsanfang' a year later. These two seem not to have travelled well, for they are seldom seen. 'Frühlingsmorgen' however, in which 'Joanna Hill' was replaced by another Hybrid Tea seedling, wins great acclaim. 'Appraising a flower spray,' writes Mr Thomas (in *Shrub Roses of Today*) 'can easily suggest that here is a rare example of the breeder's art which equals if it does not eclipse nature's best efforts.'

Kordes has also worked with the Penzance hybrid sweetbriers and the popular 'Fritz Nobis' ('Joanna Hill' x 'Magnifica'[2]) is perhaps the best known. It dates from 1940. The 'Ophelia'-shaped buds open to good clear pink semi-double flowers carried on a fine robust bush.

At the turn of the twentieth century it looked as if the lovely Rugosa roses, such as 'Blanc Double de Coubert' and 'Roseraie de l'Hay' were to be the start of numbers of robust highly scented shrub roses. Unfortunately, most of this group turned out to be sterile or nearly so and progress had to wait, as on other occasions, for a spontaneous chromosome change to occur; and to do so, most importantly, in a place where it would be appreciated.

The plant and person interaction could not have been more fortuitous. In the early 1940s and 1950s a plant of 'Max Graf' in Wilhelm Kordes' garden produced a few hips. They were gathered and their seeds sown. Only four germinated, yet the wheel of rose hybridization was moved once again.

The American 'Max Graf' is of *R. rugosa* x *R. wichuraiana* origin dating from 1919. It is a valuable ground-cover plant able to trail about, smothering weeds in its path. Of the four original seedlings one was especially fertile and its own seeds had good power of germination. This was the plant (named botanically *Rosa x kordesii* as the product of two true species) which was used as a parent of thousands of seedlings. It is apt to be overlooked that when a rose is bred and introduced it is usually the prime selection from a host of less satisfactory siblings which have to be discarded. Here the first *R. kordesii* hybrids selected for distribution in 1954 were the red 'Hamburger Phoenix' and the pale yellow 'Leverkusen'. This latter has the *wichuraiana* hybrid 'Golden Glow' as its other parent.

Subsequently, with Polypoms as the pollen parent, Kordes brought out 'Wilhelm Hausmann' and the deep pink 'Ritter von Barmstede'; 'Park-direktor Riggers' is a strong blood red. All these *kordesii* hybrids are of climbing habit, thirteen to sixteen feet in height and the later ones have a remontancy the earlier selections lack.

All, too, are of exceptional hardiness, an essential attribute for success in an eastern European climate. Herr Kordes describes the production of his *kordesii* x sweetbrier hybrid 'Flammentanz' as the

> culmination of my efforts to obtain large-bloomed crimson sweetbrier hybrids. Hardiness has always been

> one of my requirements – but all really hardy sweetbrier hybrids bloom only in May and June, make large bushes, but never have a flower in autumn.
>
> Here in this cross we broke down the resistance and now have a repeat flowerer, 'Flammentanz' … perhaps one of the most frost-hardy of all roses.

These last groups of roses have concentrated to some extent upon one breeder who has in fact been extremely catholic in his choice of pollen and seed parents. It indicates ways in which, in the search for definite attributes in garden roses, fortunate chance has to combine with endless care in planning, recording and much hard labour. Most of these *kordesii* roses are of considerable size; plants for walls or for making huge heaps of growth in big gardens. It might be suitable therefore to turn to the other end of the scale to consider what roses have been developed for the smallest gardens. These are the Miniature roses.

Sydenham Edward's *Botanical Register* of 1821 (a rival to Curtis's *Botanical Magazine* for which Edwards had earlier drawn for years) has a charming plate made at Colvill's nursery in the King's Road, Chelsea, London, of a tiny pink rose with a description:

> A very low compact, little shrub, rarely exceeding a foot in height … Mr Sweet introduced it from Mauritius (Isle of France), some years ago, and it may be the *Rosa*

> *pusilla* of the catalogue of the Botanic Garden there. China is probably its native country ... the species was named by Mr Sweet in the *Hortus Suburbanus Londinensis* in compliment to Miss Lawrence, the fair artist by whom 'The Collection of Roses from Nature,' with 90 plates was executed.

Miss Lawrence's publication of 1799 was the first work devoted to roses, so it is apt that she should be rosaceously commemorated. Surprisingly, Hurst (1941) states that the Fairy Rose, Dwarf Pink China or *R. roulettii* as it is variously known, actually originated as a sport from Parson's Pink China at Colvill's nursery. But both Ellen Willmott (*The Genus Rosa*) and Ann Wylie (*Royal Horticultural Society Journal,* 1954) accept Mauritian origin. No doubt, as the former remarks, it was 'much developed in all its parts, probably by the art of some Chinese or Japanese cultivator'.

Although in the early nineteenth century there was sufficient interest in the Fairy rose for Paul's *Rose Garden* (9th edition) to list nine varieties, it is most logical to discuss it here. For it was not until the later twentieth century that gardeners have been enthusiastic enough (probably in response to ever smaller gardens), and breeders sufficiently sure of their market, for a range of miniature roses to make their appearance. Parents have lately not been restricted to *R. lawrenceana*; among others, the 'Old Blush' China has also been used and the claims has even been made that 'Juliette' is a miniature sport from the highly robust Bourbon-type 'Grüss an Teplitz.'

They are now to be found in almost as wide a colour range as are Hybrid Teas or Floribundas which, on a miniature scale, they resemble. While the typical height is close to that of the original Fairy rose, different cultivars can vary from under four up to eight inches in height. The Spanish breeder Pedro Dot who, in addition to de Vink of the Netherlands, has done most to diversify this group, has with 'Tí' produced the ultimate in miniature roses. It flowers at a height of two inches. Although needing careful use in the garden, the charm of these little plants is undeniable. They are not diminutives with full-size blooms (a fact which makes bonsai trees in flower seem out of balance) but perfectly proportioned in all their parts: fairies in fact, not dwarves.

Just as in the past a species gave rise to just one or two forms, mutants or chance seedlings, so in the twentieth century did some splendid individualists occur. Sometimes their parentage is known from their raisers' careful documentation, sometimes, while one parent is obvious (usually of course the seed parent), the other can only be guessed at. This is nowhere more apparent than among climbing roses. It has already been seen how various of the oriental *synstylae* were brought into cultivation at the turn of the nineteenth and twentieth centuries and were quickly used in the production of hybrids, how many of the originally bush Hybrid Tea and Floribunda varieties produced climbing mutants, and how more recently the Rugosa and Eglanteria hybrids were poured into the same melting pot with surprising amalgams coming out.

Occasionally still, in spite of further efforts, a species refuses to move further. The beauties of *R. bracteata*, the Macartney Rose, have already been extolled (page 102), yet, after two hundred admired years in cultivation, only one hybrid, and that with an unknown Hybrid Tea, is at all known. However, to be responsible for one child of supreme beauty may be preferable to the promiscuous production of bevies of brats. 'Mermaid' is that supreme beauty which William Paul raised as long ago as 1918. It has the excessively thorny wood of its known parent and even more vigour; in a warm climate it can reach a great size, flinging out trails of four-inch-wide soft yellow flowers for months on end.

Similarly sized, creamy white flowers in incredible profusion are the feature of 'Nevada,' of even more doubtful parentage. Pedro Dot brought it out in 1927, stating it to be 'a Giralda' (H.T.) x *R. moyesii*, but, while habit and freedom of flower support that species, cytological information causes doubt. Nonetheless 'Nevada' is rightly one of the most popular shrub roses of the twentieth century – even without a scent. In 1959 its pink sport named 'Marguerite Hilling' was introduced.

Two further fine modern roses of very different type

can be chosen from the annually increasing number of hybrids to indicate the diversity of both breeders and breeding. David Austin is the raiser of 'Constance Spry.' Introduced in 1961, this is an old Gallica crossed with one of the many Floribundas of the 1930s. An unlikely pairing, perhaps, but the product is splendid, combining in one rose some of the best virtues of the old and new. His later English roses have changed the face of the rose garden.

From the huge house of Kordes has come 'Cerise Bouquet,' dating from 1958. Here the old 'Crimson Glory' has been combined with another of those western Chinese species, *R. multibracteata*, brought in at the turn of the century. Again an unexpected combination which has produced a strong arching plant of great originality, with the grey-green curtain effect of the species studded with clusters of loosely double cerise-red flowers.

One further rose and its still-developing potential demands discussion. There have been passing references earlier in this book to the fabled Rose of Persia, *Hulthemia persica*. Is it or is it not a true rose? Is this the plant which shares Minoan walls at Knossos with the saffron-gatherer and the Young Prince? A more profitable question in the context of this chapter is whether the plant of undoubted beauty has anything to offer to the twenty-first-century rose garden.

While the species has been known since the 1790s it has never been successfully cultivated for long except in hot, well-drained positions that resemble its semi-desert home. Only one hybrid, until the last decade, has with any certainty been grown. This is *Hulthemosa hardii* (or *Rosa x hardii*) which appeared by chance in Paris in 1836 at the gardens of the Luxembourg Palace, whose then curator, M Hardy, is commemorated. The other parent is *R. clinophylla*, a member of the widely separated *Bracteatae* group. This hybrid, though not an easy plant to grow, is less difficult than the Persian parent and, because it retains those striking red-blotched flowers, has been cultivated with care ever since.

The story now moves forward with the well-known rose breeder, Jack Harkness of Hitchin in Hertfordshire, who obtained seed of the wild Iranian plant in 1967. Germination of Hulthemia is rapid, and growth, under glass, is quick. A few flowers had been produced by the following year and these were immediately used at the start of a unique hybridization programme.

As this progressed it was found that using Hulthemia pollen on other roses, even those with the necessary diploid chromosome number for successful nuclear fusion, brought no results. Hulthemia had continually to be the seed parent. In 1970 twenty-seven seedlings of *H. persica* x R. 'Canary Bird' (see page 64) germinated and six more of which 'Ballerina' was pollen parent ('Ballerina') is a post-Pemberton Hybrid Musk). All the 'Canary Bird' hybrids and one of the 'Ballerina' batch were grown to flowering and proved to maintain the distinctive red Hulthemia petal blotch, though in differing amounts. Flower size was increased on those of Hulthemia by half. The leaves were all compound and stipules were present, the effect of 'Canary Bird.' Although Dr Roberts of the North East London Polytechnic tried 'by various means to double the chromosome complement in an attempt to produce a fertile allotetrapolid', crosses with Hulthemia had to be restricted to other diploids. Nonetheless, considerable diversity, such is the range or roses, was possible. Further pollen parents were 'Buff Beauty,' 'Cornelia' (Hybrid Musks), 'Trier' (Hybrid Musk with a Noisette and *R. multiflora* ancestry), *R. chinensis mutabilis,* 'Phyllis Bide', 'Margo Koster' and, perhaps more excitingly, 'Mermaid'. The connection here with *H.* x *hardii* and 'Mermaid,' both having a *Bracteateae* parent, will not have been overlooked.

More than 1,000 crosses, producing on average little over two seeds at a time, were made from 1968 to 1975. From these, seventy-four hybrids germinated of which fifty-three grew to maturity. A second generation of *Hulthemia persica* x *(H. persica* X 'Canary Bird') now exists, but the coveted fertile hybrid is still elusive.

The end of this story is yet to be written; no doubt it will hold disappointments, surprises and, it is hoped, for those who devote years to the work, real and lasting rewards.

[1] Graham Stuart Thomas, *Shrub Roses Today*, 1962.

[2] A Penzance seedling.

CHAPTER 8

THE ROSE CONSUMED

Some of the most fascinating rose lore is contained in the early texts, which combine – in a period when those sciences were virtually inseparable – botany and medicine. Early classifications of many plants, including roses, were based in many instances less upon visual characteristics than upon the virtues, real or imagined, of the plants concerned.

Perfumes made from roses have existed since classical times and we can understand how, when medicaments were not only hit-and-miss affairs but usually unpleasant to take, any agreeable additive would be valuable. Rosewater is known to have been made from the early ninth century AD and throughout the Middle Ages it was made in ever increasing quantities.

In English, Turner, Gerard, Parkinson and Culpeper (the most extravagant of all in his claims for the medical efficacy of plant cures) can be consulted for rose use.

Elizabeth Blackwell's *A Curious Herbal* (1737/82),[1] however, gives the true early flavour without excessive prolixity. In the 1730s Mrs Blackwell took a house in Swan Walk, Chelsea, overlooking the Physic Garden, in order to draw specimens from that garden. The reason for her labours was to raise money to get her husband out of a debtors' prison (the story is a confused and bizarre one: eventually Dr Blackwell was beheaded in Sweden). Mrs Blackwell's work was published in two fine folios under the title *A Curious Herbal*, every four plates being prefixed by a page describing their virtues.

One of the rose plates, named *R. rubra*, is of particular interest as being the type-portrait of what, due to rules of nomenclatural precedence, is now known as *R. gallica*. Of this Mrs Blackwell writes:

> The Red rose is more binding and restringent than any of the Other Species, and are esteemed good in all kinds of Fluxes. They strengthen the Stomach, prevent vomiting, stop tickling Coughs by preventing the Defluxion of Rheum, and are of great service in consumption. The Apices are also accounted cordial.

Nine preparations are subsequently listed, from simple rosewater to unguents and tinctures. Apices are presumably the shoot tips (certainly the young shoots of the sweetbrier *R. eglanteria* can be peeled and then candied by simmering in sugar syrup).

R. x *alba* is briefly described, as is the Damask rose:

> The Flowers are of a gentle cathartic Nature, purging choleric and serious Humors. They are frequently given to children and weakly Persons, mixt into stronger Cathartics.

But it is *R. canina* which brings on the lady's keen sense of plagiarism and shows that popular medicine in the Age of Reason had not moved far from the all-accepting semi-witchcraft of earlier centuries.

> The flowers of this Rose are thought more Restringent than ye Garden: some look upon them as a specific for ye excess of ye Catamenia. The Pulp of ye Hips strengthens ye Stomach, cools the heat of Fevers, is pectoral, good for coughs, spitting of Blood and ye Scurvy. The Seed is good against ye Stone and Gravel. The Bedeguar is said to have the same virtues. The official Preparation is, the Conserva Cynosbati.

The bedeguar referred to is the type of rose gall often called rose pincushion. Culpeper, writing in the previous century and devoting two and a half closely packed pages to the treatments for which roses were used, from strengthening of the gums to venereal diseases, also refers to these galls:

> ...In the middle of the balls are often found certain white worms, which being dried and made into powder, and some of it drank, is found by experience of many to kill and drive forth the worms of the belly.

But as he has already explained, before choosing any medicine one must:

> consider what planet causeth the disease ... by what planet the afflicted part of the body is governed ...

Much of Culpeper's information on roses is a direct crib from Parkinson's *Theatrum Botanicum* of 1610, to which he added those astrological obsessions of his own. Parkinson, by comparison, while describing the optimistic cures of his time shows nonetheless a proper caution:

> Pliny setteth downe in his eighth book and fourth Chapter that the roote of the wilde Rose is singular good to cure the biting of a mad Dogge, which as he saith, (but how wee may beleeve him I know not) was found out by a miracle.

There are some odd ideas too in the early nineteenth century:

> Receipt for sore Eyes
> Take Conserve of red Roses two Ounces, the finest Bole Armoniac half an Ounce, and Sugar of Lead a Dram; then add as much Frogs Spawn Water as will make it of a proper Consistence, and with this anoint the Eyes when going to Bed.
>
> (From *The British Housewife or the Cook Housekeeper's and Gardiner's Companion* by Mrs Martha Bradley)

And, a little later, in 1847, Samuel B. Parsons wrote:

> Honey of roses is made by beating up rose petals with a very small portion of boiling water; the liquid, after being filtered, is boiled with honey. This is esteemed for sore throats, for ulcers in the mouth, and for anything that is benefitted by the use of honey.

Rose products have, fortunately, been as much used to enhance the healthy as to cure the sick. Though not considered now as food, rose petals cooked or raw were once part of many puddings. Rosewater too was then more widely used in cooking. Frequently, too, in the late Middle Ages roses and 'rede rose' petals were used as a final garnish before the dish was 'served forthe.'

John Gerard suggests the following for a conserve of roses:

> Take Roses at your pleasure, put them to boyle in faire water having regard to the quantity; for if you have many Roses you may take more water, if fewer, the lesse water will serve; the which you shall boyle at the least three or foure houres, even as you would boile a piece of meate, untill in the eating they be very tender, at which time, the Roses will lose their colour, that you would thinke your labour lost, and the thing spoiled. But proceed, for though the Roses have lost their colour, the water hath gotten the tincture there; then shall you adde unto one pound of Roses, four pound of fine sugar in pure pouder, and so according to the rest of the Roses. Thus shall you let them boyle gently after the sugar is put therto; continually stirring it with a woodden Spatula until it be cold, whereof one pound weight is worth sex pound of the crude or raw conserve, as well for the vertues and goodnesse in taste, as also for the beautifull colour.

Sir Hugh Plat was a contemporary of Gerard's and, five years after the publication of the *Herball* in 1587, Plat brought out *The Jewel House of Art and Nature*. Here he describes how to produce 'Rose-water and Rose-vinegar of the colour of the Rose';

> If you would make your Rose-water and Rose-vinegar, of a Rubic colour, than make choyce of the crimson velvet coloured leaves, clipping away the white with a

paire of sheers; and being thorow dryed, put a good large handfull of them into a pint of Damask or red Rose-water: stop your glasse well and set it in the sunne till you see the leaves have lost their colour: or, for more expedition, you may perform this work in *balneo* in a few hours; and when you take out the old leaves you may put in fresh, till you find the colour to please you. Keepe this Rose-water in the glasses very well stopt, and the fuller the better. What I have said of Rose-water, the same may also be intended of Rose-vinegar, but the whiter vinegar you chuse for the purpose the colour therof will be the better.

'Take roses at your pleasure …' (see opposite)

Sir Hugh also gives a recipe for preserving whole roses:

> Dip a Rose that is neither in the bud, nor over-blowne, in a sirup, consisting of sugar, double-refined, and Rose-water boiled to his full height, then open the leaves one by one with a fine bodkin either of bone or wood; and presently, if it be a hot, sunny day, and whillest the sunne is in some good height, lay them in papers in the sunne, or else dry them with some gentle heat in a close room, heating the room before you set them in, or in an oven upon papers, in pewter dishes, and then put them up in glasses; and keepe them in dry cupboards neere the fire: you must take out the seeds, if you meene to eat them. You may proove this preserving with sugar-candy instead of sugar if you please.

These crystalized roses are obviously meant more for garnishing than consumption, hence the warning about removing the hard central ovary. Crystalizing petals alone is a safer method:

> Beat up ½ teaspoon of cold water to the white of an egg. Dip fresh rose petals first into the white and then into caster sugar. Lay on waxed paper in the sun to dry. They may be eaten at once or stored in an airtight tin for later use.

A more complicated, unusual and differently motivated rose preservation recipe is described by Fynes Morison in his *Itinerary* of 1605. Here in *Travels in Bohemia* the social nuances of who wears roses and when is minutely observed:

> For they keepe Roses all winter in little pots of earth, whereof they open one each Saturday at night and distribute the Roses among the women of the house, to the very kitchen maids; others keep them all in one pot, and weekly take as many Roses as they neede, and cover the rest, keeping them fresh till the next summer. And the common sort mingle guilded nutmegs with these roses, and make garlands thereof: Only women weare these Garlands in winter, but in summer time men of the better sort weare them within doors, and men of the common sort weare them going abroade. They keepe Roses all winter in this sort, they choose the closest and thickest buds of all kindes of Roses, but the Damaske Roses best keepe the smell, and other kindes the colour. Then they take a pot of earth, and sprinckle some bay salt in the bottome, and lay these buds severally, not very close one to the other, in two rowes one above the other, which done they sprinckle the same, and wet all the buds with two little glasses of Rhenish wine, and againe sprinckle them with bay salt in greater quantity, yet such as it may not eate the leaves. In like sort they put up each two rowes of buds, till the pot be full, which

Rosa Damascena.
Rosier de Cels.

Rosa bifera officinalis.
Rosier des Parfumeu

Rosa Sulfurea.
Rosier jaune de

> they cover with wood or leade, so as no aire can enter, and they lay it up in a cold cellar, where no sun comes. When they take out the buds, they dip them in lukewarm water, put them in the oven when the bread is taken out which makes the leaves open with the turning of the buds betweene two fingers, then they dip a feather in Rhenish wine, and wipe the leaves therewith, to refresh the colour, and some doe the like with rose-water, to renew the smell.

It is doubtful if this has been recently attempted and, to be frank, the method does not attract by its practicability. Yet there is such circumstantial description that one has no doubt that Mr Morison fully believed what he was told. But was he there for the whole process and the exhumation of the roses? The use of Rhenish wine as a sort of elixir of life is an attractive thought.

Nowadays it is always possible to wear fresh roses even in the depths of winter, but these products of the glasshouse lack the lush savour of the natural summer blooms. The scent is best preserved for winter in potpourri, for which Sir Hugh Plat again offers a preliminary; rose leaves, of course, are petals:

> You must in rose-time make choice of such roses as are either in the bud, nor full blowne which you must specially cull and chuse from the rest, then take sand and drie it thoroughly well, and having shallow boxes, make first an

> even lay of sand, upon which lay your rose-leaves one by one (so as none of them touch other). Set this box in some warme, sunny place in a hot sunny day (and commonly in two hot sunny dayes they will be thorow dry), an thus you may have rose-leaves and other flowers to lay about your basons, windows, etc., all the winter long.

Here is one of the many modern variants on the potpourri theme:

> Cut your roses when the dew has dried and the warm sun has brought out their scent but not yet begun to fade them. Separate the petals from the centres and sprinkle lightly with salt. Dry thoroughly spread on paper in an airy room. Make a well balanced blend by using light-scented tea-rose petals with some fuller bodied scent. Other scented flowers and leaves can be added.
> Now take ½ oz each of cloves, mace, cinnamon, allspice, crushed coriander and cardomom seeds and 1 oz each of gum storax and gum bensoin and a little salt. Add the spice mixture gradually so as to stop before it dominates the rose perfume. When thoroughly blended sprinkle with a little alcohol and keep pot-pourri in tightly stopped jars, stirring occasionally, for 4–5 weeks.[2]

It is now possible to obtain proprietary 'potpourri makers' which are a combination of spices and preservatives to which one adds the flowers._Whatever method is used it must be remembered that potpourri left for long periods in open bowls is bound to lose much of its perfume. Also, a constant scent becomes less and less noticed; it is better to put some out at intervals and to warm the jar before the lid is removed.

There are many recipes for encapsulating the scent of summer roses into the flavour of a conserve. In Bunyard's seminal *Old Garden Roses* (1936) are the following directions:

> Rose jelly is the simplest of rose confections, and within the capacity of all jam makers. Windfalls, or the peeling and cores of apples, are covered with water, and simmered as for apple jelly, with a handful of red or cottage roses to every pint of water. After simmering, the flavoured juice is strained off on to another handful of petals, and left for the rest of the day and the night to infuse. Next day, or even the day after, it is measured, and put into a skillet with a fresh handful of leaves. Three-quarters of a pound of sugar is measured for every pint of juice, and this sugar is made hot while the infusion comes to the boil. The hot sugar is then added, and the contents of the skillet boiled quickly until the jelly sheets from the spoon, or two drips on the spoon run together and hang. The juice of half a lemon may be added for each pint as it comes to the boil, if the sharpness is liked. The jelly is strained through clean butter muslin (which has been scalded and wrung out), poured into small jars, and tied down at once.

Rose-petal syrup, surprisingly, does not use the petals fresh:

> Select fresh, unbruised petals; carefully separate and spread on clean cloth or screen to dry for 1 to 2 days. When at least a quart of rose petals have been dried, press them tightly together between the palms of your hands. Place the carefully pressed petals in a heavy enamel pan. Barely cover petals with water, measuring as you go. Bring to the boiling and gradually add 3 cups sugar for each cup of water used. Boil slowly 10 minutes or until syrup is formed. Strain through filter cloth, bottle, cork tightly and keep two weeks before using.

The syrup is used to flavour custards, fruit drinks, puddings and fruit salads to taste.

The trouble with jams and syrups is that they are only additives (except in the Middle East where a lone spoonful of jam is frequently offered with a drink). Rose wine therefore is a way of concentrating the flavour.

Sir Hugh Plat also writes:

> Also if you ferment the juice of Roses onely, without any leaves mixed therein, you may draw an excellent spirit from the same; or if you keep the juyce of damask roses onely in close vessels well seasoned with the rose, it will yield a delicate spirit, after it hath wrought itself to a sufficient head by the inward rotation or circulation of nature …

But it is wise to take a modern recipe for more certain success in wine-making:

> Pour eight pints of boiling water on to two pints highly scented dark red rose petals and macerate them with a wooden spoon. Cover and soak for two days, macerating twice daily. Strain and press the petals and stir in 1 lb grape juice concentrate, 2 lb of sugar, ½ oz of acid blend, half teaspoon of tannin and some yeast nutrient.
>
> Ferment to specific gravity 1.016. After racking into a clean container, two crushed Campden tablets are added to terminate fermentation. A suitably rosé-type wine is made with white grape-juice.

From *The British Housewife or the Cook Housekeeper's and Gardiner's Companion* by Mrs Martha Bradley comes:

> *To Make Rossoly, the true Italian Receipt*
>
> Gather fresh Damask Roses, Orange Flowers, Jessamy Flowers, Cloves and July Flowers; pick them clean, set on some water to boil, when it has boiled well, let it stand to cool a little. Put these clean Flowers into a China Bason, pour the Water upon them when it is no hotter than to bear the Finger in it, then cover it up, and let it stand three Hours.
>
> Gently pour all into a fine Linnen Bag, and let the Water run off without squeezing the Flowers. To a Pint

of this Water add a Quart of fine Melasses Spirit, and half a Pint of strong Cinnamon Water; add three Tea Spoonfuls of Essence of Amber-grease, and stir all well together. This is the true Italian Rossoly.

In the following recipe the acute accent somewhat alters the meaning of rose, but this delicious pudding just qualifies for inclusion here.

Rosé Syllabub

Stir together the juice and the finely grated rind of a lemon with four tablespoons of rosé wine and 3 oz of castor sugar. Leave overnight. Fold in ½ pint of double cream and add a touch of pink colouring. Whisk the mixture and put into individual glasses; strew with crystallized rose petals.

Many recipes use commercially produced rosewater instead of fresh rose petals: here are two cakes, one from the seventeenth century and the other some two hundred years later.

Princess Elizabeth Rose-Flavoured Cake

To make a cake with Rose-water, the way of the royal princess, the lady Elizabeth, daughter to King Charles I. Take half a peck of Flowre, half a pint of Rose-water, a pint of Ale yeast, a pint of Cream, boyl it, a pound and a half of Butter, six eggs (leave out the whites), four

> pound of Currants, one half pound of sugar, one Nutmeg, and a little salt, work it very well and let it stand half an hour by the fire, and then work it again, and then make it up and let it stand an hour and a halfe in the oven; let not your Oven be too hot.
>
> (quoted in *The Rose Anthology* by H. L.V. Fletcher)

Mrs Martha Bradley provides the second:

> *To make a Shrewsbery Cake*
>
> Take four Eggs, beat them with two Spoonfuls of Rose Water, and three of Sack, one Pound of Flour well dried, half a Pound of Sugar, and three Quarters of a Pound of Butter.
>
> Cut your Butter in Slices upon the Flour, and put it to your Sugar, then put your Eggs to the Flour, Sugar and Butter, and mix them all well together.
>
> Then make it into Cakes of the Bigness you chuse, as thick as a Crown Piece; Rosel them like the Lid of a Pie, and bake them in a slow Oven.

The bases of most modern rose perfumes are attar of roses and its rosewater by-product, which are produced in large quantities in, especially, Bulgaria (see page 213). But no doubt every rose-growing country has its own vernacular methods and used for rose-based cosmetics.

For whitening an unfashionably red complexion Robert Burton, in The Anatomy of Melancholy recommends:

> … And withal to refrigerate the face, by washing it often with rose, violet, nenuphar, lettuce, borage waters and the like … Quercetan, *spagir phar.* cap 6 commends the water of frogs' spawn for ruddiness in the face. Crato, *consil. 283 Scolizii* would fain have them use all summer the condite flowers of succory, strawberry-water, roses …
>
> It is good overnight to anoint the face with hare's blood, and in the morning to wash it with strawberry and cowslip water, the juice of distilled lemons, juice of cucumbers, or to use the seeds of melons, or kernels of peaches beaten small, or the roots of arum, and mingled with wheat-bran to bake it in an oven, and to crumble it in strawberry-water etc. or to put fresh cheese-curds to a red face.

A simple home-made rosewater maintains the authentic savour of the rose, not least because of its freshness:

> Rosewater can be freshly made very day during the season and it is very fragrant and pleasant to wash in. Gather at least 2 lb. rose petals and cover them with water, preferably rainwater. The water should only just cover the petals. Bring slowly to the boil and then simmer for a few minutes. This water keeps good for two days. *(The Rose Anthology)*

But for a lasting rose perfume, preserving ingredients must be added, as Mrs Bradley describes:

The following pages show plates 15–18

A Receipt to make Perfumes
Take two Ounces of red Rose Buds (the leaves of them must be stripped off) and use only the red part of the Flower.

Pound them in a Mortar, and put to them an Ounce of Benjamin: When you have pounded them small together, put in three Grains of Civet, four of Ambergrease, and twelve of Musk; Mix these with your Fingers, and when you have mixed them well, make them up in little Cakes.

In the making them up you must put a little Flour in the palm of your Hand, only to make them hang together; so let them dry in a Window.

A modern recipe in this line also reaches back to the origins of the rosary (see page 45) in which knots in the string or stones of the chaplet are replaced by beads made of rose petals. Such beads, it might be said, if made into a regular rosary sequence, tend to compound the virtues:

To make a double strand necklace of rose beads you need the following ingredients:
3 cups finely chopped scented rose (I used Dr Van Fleet)
1¾ cups flour
4 tablespoons salt
water
10 drops rose geranium oil
oil paint, if desired.

Combine the flour and salt, mixing in just enough water to moisten the flour into a thick paste. Press the finely chopped rose petals into this mixture. Finally mix in the rose geranium oil and red or yellow oil paint if you wish. The oil paint creates a beautiful soft color in what otherwise would be dark beads.

The beads can them be formed and strung on a florists' wire to dry. After they have dried completely you can string them on nylon cord available at most jewelry stores. Some helpful hints:

1. When adding the oil paint keep in mind that the beads will dry several shades lighter than they appear when wet.
2. The bead dough tends to be very soft and sticky. It sometimes helps to spread the mixture on a cookie sheet to dry a little. Then make your beads allowing them to dry a little also, so they won't lose their shape when you put them on the florist's wire. (The weather affects this. On a dry day they would be much easier to work with.)
3. The dough can be kept in the refrigerator in plastic wrap for a week or more, if you do not have time to form all the beads.
4. After the beads are dry you can add to their fragrance by placing several drops of rose geranium oil in a jar, roll the jar to coat it with oil, put the beads in and cover the jar. This can also be done if the beads begin to lose their fragrance with use.[3]

And so the lists can go on: variants on the wines, cakes, cosmetic preparations which have been given here as well as rose-vinegar, rose-honey, rose-jams and rose-almost-anything-you-will. All, if not life-supporting, are most certainly life-enhancing. The folk recipes do not as a rule require any particular type of rose; so long as it is highly scented an ancestral species is as acceptable as the latest Hybrid-Tea – or the other way round.

In the commercial production of rose preparations, however, as with other plants of use to man, selections have been made which are known to be most productive. Thus the enormous industry that flourished over the centuries at Provins, south-east of Paris, was based on *R. gallica officinalis*. This rose has the invaluable ability of holding its scent when dried or even, as some claim, appearing then to increase its fragrance. The dried petals can be sold as such and, especially in the past when communications were difficult, transported slowly for the subsequent production of medicaments and cordials, wines and sweetmeats.

In Britain a similar, though smaller, rose industry flourished up to the beginning of this century. Dr Septimus Piesse (in *The Art of Perfumery*, 4th edition, 1879) writes:

> Roses are cultivated to a large extent in England near Mitcham in Surrey for perfumers' use, to make rose-water. In the season … about the end of June … they are gathered as soon as the dew is off and sent to

> London in sacks. When they arrive, they are immediately spread out upon a cool floor; otherwise, if left in a heap, they heat to such an extent, in two or three hours, as to be quite spoiled. There is no organic matter which so rapidly absorbs oxygen, and becomes heated spontaneously, as a mass of freshly-gathered roses.
>
> To preserve these roses, the London perfumers immediately pickle them; for this purpose, the leaves are separated from the stalks, and to every bushel of flowers, equal to about 6 lbs in weight, 1 lb of common salt is thoroughly rubbed in. The salt absorbs the water existing in the petals, and rapidly becomes brine, reducing the whole to a pasty mass, which is finally stowed away in casks. In this way they will keep almost any length of time, without the fragrance being seriously injured. A good Rose-water can be prepared by distilling 12 lbs of pickled roses, and $2^1/_2$ gallons of water.

But clearly, commercial rose production is at the climatic limit of its range in England; higher quality rose products are more cheaply produced in warmer areas. Dr Piesse goes on, rather sadly:

> The rose-water that is imported from the South of France is, however, very superior in odour to any that can be produced here. As it is a residuary product of the

> distillation of roses for procuring the otto [attar], it has a richness of aroma which appears to be inimitable with English-grown roses.

The other vital point is that the attar of roses industry is based not upon the Provins rose but on forms of *R. damascena*. Although a small amount of attar of roses is still produced at Grasse in the South of France, the main area of world production became the district of Kazanlik, Bulgaria. At the time, being a Communist country, this became a state-controlled industry, which would have upset the worthy Dr Piesse. He remarks, somewhat xenophobically, that:

> Had not the first Russian aggression been 'nipped in the bud' ... it is nearly certain that the scene of war (in 1854) would have been laid out not in the Crimea, but in the Rose Farms of the Balkans; nevertheless, who is there would have doubted the prowess of the descendants of the Houses of York and Lancaster?

Be that as it may, the Bulgarian industry began in the early eighteenth century and had gone from strength to strength in the particularly favourable local conditions. Although modern methods of growing have been adopted, those harvesting the crop have no choice but to follow the precedents of their forebears. The opening flowers contain most oil at daybreak and must be gathered within a couple of hours, for the oil becomes dispersed as the sun gathers strength.

In rose flowers this volatile oil is secreted into oil cells, secretion ducts and into glandular hairs. But unlike most of the oils obtained from flowers which are used in perfumery, attar of roses is obtained by distillation (the others are made by enfleurage, using warm wax). Nonetheless, the method has some disadvantages. Dry overheating leads to a loss of, or to undesirable changes in, odour, so that most modern stills employ steam. So important is it for the fresh flowers to be processed without delay that distillation is frequently carried out in the field where the roses are gathered.

Flowers are placed on a perforated tray in a vessel through which the steam is passed. The oil also becomes vaporized and the two vapours are condensed by cooling. They are collected in a Florentine receiver; this has an outlet near the top through which the floating oil (being lighter than water and immiscible with it) is run off, and an outlet near the bottom for the water. This is usually redistilled and can still be sufficiently fragrant to be sold as rose-water in the way that Dr Piesse refers to. The attar is dried and stored in tightly stoppered phials. Its cost is indicated by the fact that only one part of attar is obtained from 3,000 parts of rose petals – that is, approximately 200 pounds of petals produce one ounce of rose oil.

It is interesting, and perhaps salutary, to note that

modern science has not so far succeeded in producing a synthetic oil of rose; thus, although cultivation methods and improved stills have increased the yield, the attar is still the property of the rose itself.

But it is now possible to explain the origin and behaviour of oil of rose. Many plants produce such volatile oils which consist of mixtures of monoterpene substances, derived in a specific way from several molecules of acetic acid. Monoterpenes never occur singly but in complex mixtures of closely related chemicals. These often differ from one another only by the arrangement of their constituent atoms and/or isomers. The monoterpene mixtures chiefly result from the inherent instability of the molecules. This explains, to some extent, the frequently rapid deterioration of the oils once they are removed from the plant. So, too, because they are unsaturated, oxidation can occur on exposure to air, leading to a darkening in colour and often odour change as well.

Traces of rose oil are found in many species and cultivars but economically only a couple are worth cultivating on the scale that is necessary. In Bulgaria, although *R. alba* is grown commercially on a small scale – presumably in conditions that are less suitable for the Damask because its attar production is only half as great – the main source is *R. damascena trigintipetala*. Those in the West who wish to grow the true plant can find it in the lists suitably named 'Kazanlik'.

There seems to be no definite record of the original discovery of oil of rose. Italy and Germany in the sixteenth and seventeenth centuries have been suggested as places and times, however vague. More definite, but probably allegorical, is the well-known story which gives the credit to the Persian noblewoman Nur Jehan, wife of the Moghul Emperor Jehangir, who had succeeded Akbar the great in 1605. It is said that Nur Jehan observed the fragrant oil floating on the surface of a canal in the palace garden that had been filled with rosewater and ordered it to be collected.

Such extravagance in the use of rosewater recalls the excesses of Heliogabalus and was symptomatic of that luxurious Persian way of life which Jehangir adopted upon his marriage. (He said that 'he had handed her [Nur-Jehan] the country in return for a cup of wine and a few morsels of food'.) It would thus seem likely that the origins of attar lie in Persia, rather than India, whence the Empress took it. In 1684 the German botanist Kaempfer recorded that Persian rose distilleries were flourishing and that the attar was more precious even than gold and was certainly widely sought after. This gives the impression of an industry of long standing.

While attar of roses, rosewater and their derivatives are the products of the newly opened flowers of a few species and their forms, all roses which ripen fruit have the potential to produce valuable extracts from the hips. Here is Mrs Beeton's Rose Hip Syrup:

> Boil 4 pints of water and throw in 3lbs of minced up wild rose hips. Skim once or twice as the mixture boils. Allow to cool for 15 minutes. Pass the pulp through muslin twice. Keep the liquid and boil up the pulp again with 2 further pints of water. Treat as before. Return both extracted liquids to the pan and boil till the juice is reduced to about 3 pints. Sweeten, stirring well and pour into warmed bottles. Store in a dark cupboard.

Mrs Beeton also offers a Rose Hip Jelly; the method is modernized in this version:

> Choose firm but well-ripened fruit. Wash and top and tail. Use 2 lbs of hips to $1\frac{1}{2}$ pints water and pressure cook for 30 minutes. Push through wire sieve and strain again through a jelly bag. Add 1lb sugar and $\frac{1}{2}$ teaspoon of tartaric acid to each pint of juice. Return to heat in open cooker to dissolve sugar and boil until setting point is reached.

There is no suggestion in the recipe of any particular value of rose-hip syrup – it is just another pleasant fruit flavouring for drinks or adding to jellies and other desserts. But during World War II the syrup was a vital source of vitamin C to beleaguered Britain. It had been found in 1934 that wild rose hips contained twenty times as much vitamin C as oranges and four times as much as blackcurrants – in fact more than any other fruit.

From 1941 national collections of rose hips were made each autumn, increasing in amount from 120 tons to an average by the end of the war of 450. Rose hips continued to be collected, especially by children, and sold to commercial manufacturers of syrup: seventy mg of vitamin C per fluid ounce is expected. It is interesting to note that this must be one of the few economically viable products from entirely wild material collected by a basically industrial country.

Even Dioscorides, in the first century AD, suggested a medicinal virtue for rose hips (his wild rose being most probably *R. sempervirens)*. Here he is in the first English translation by John Goodyers (1652–55):

> The fruit thereof being dryed stops the belly (the lanuginous stuff thereof being taken out for thus is naught for the Asteric) it being made hot in wine, and dranck.

We note that the hair-covered seeds are considered dangerous if taken.

This point is repeated in the Medical Botany (1793) of Dr William Woodville. What is a surprise is that by the late eighteenth century the hips were considered of no practical medical value:

> The fruit called heps or hips, has a sourish taste, and obtains a place in the London Pharmacopoeia in the form of a conserve; for this purpose the seeds and chaffy fibres are to be carefully removed; for if these prickly

> fibres are not entirely scraped off from the internal surface of the hips, the conserve is liable to produce considerable irritation on the primae viae. This official preparation of the fruit is not supposed to possess any medical virtue (formerly, however, it was esteemed useful in many disorders, as dropsies, calculous complaints, Dysentries, haemorrhages etc.), but it is agreeable to the taste, and well suited to give form to the more active articles of the *Materia Medica.*

Of course any ripe fruit is grist to the mill of home wine makers. And rose hips are used to produce both dry table wine and dessert wine.

This is the table wine from B. C. A. Turner's *Wine-making*, 1965:

> Wash and crush 3 litres of ripe rose-hips and 250 gms sultanas and pour on 4 litres of boiling water. When cool add the juice and rind of a large lemon, one Campden tablet and some pectic enzyme. Cover and leave for 24 hours before stirring in 1 kg of sugar and sauterne yeast and nutrient. Ferment for 5 days. This is then strained and fermentation is continued under an airlock until specific gravity 1.010 is reached.
>
> The wine is racked off into corked bottles and stored in the dark, to preserve the delicate colour, for ideally at least one year.

Perhaps this should be drunk by keen rosarians in winter, as they read through the catalogues and order even more bushes from the growers.

[1] *Botanicum Officinale; or a Curious Herbal: Giving an Account of all such plants as are now used in the practice of Physick. With their Descriptions and Virtues*, 1722.

[2] Adapted from Peter Coats, *Roses.*

[3] Betty Westlake, *Potomac Herb Journal*, vol. viii, no. 3

CHAPTER 10

THE ROSE EXTOLLED

For us the rose from year to year renews in abundance
The yellow stamens of its crimson flower.
Far and away the best of all in power and fragrance
It colours the oil which bears its name.
No man can say, No man remember, how many used there are
For Oil of Roses as a cure for mankind's ailments.

This transcription and translation by Raef Payne from the original Latin hexameters of Walahfrid Strabo seems to predate by some 1200 years those not dissimilar lines by Walter de la Mare:

No one knows
Through what wild centuries
Roves back the Rose

which appear to be of almost obligatory use in every book on roses. In both, the feeling of the ultimate mystery of the origin of the rose is combined with the certainty that man and rose have always existed, since time began, in an almost symbiotic relationship.

Walahfrid's collection of poems, *Hortulus,* or *The Little Garden* was written around the year AD 840 and, although no longer existing in the author's hand, a manuscript of twenty-five years later lay unconsidered in the library of the Benedictine monastery of St Gall until the early sixteenth century.

It remains the earliest surviving piece of horticultural literature. In the foreword to the Hunt Botanical Library facsimile edition (1966) quoted here, the director, G. H. M. Lawrence states:

> It has survived this long, and should live for more than as long again, not because of its gardening innovation, accounts of new plants, or pharmacological discoveries reported in it, but because it is beautiful poetry, because it is full of man's love for the earth and for the plants he grows in it. It is pure gardening literature, not on herbal nor on agricultural account.

Its writer, Walahfrid the Squint-eyed (which is what 'Strabo' means), entered the Benedictine monastery of Reichnau on Lake Constance when he was only eight years old. After a highly adventurous life, he became Abbot of Reichnau and died by drowning when still only forty years old. Not long before, it seems, the twenty-seven short poems which make up the *Hortulus* were written. They celebrate many plants: sage and southernwood, chervil and clary and, of course, the lily and the rose. They also pronounce anathema upon nettles. And it is suitable to begin a highly selective account of references to the rose in literature with one that talks to us so clearly across the centuries, albeit from those so-called 'Dark Ages'.

Moving into symbolism Walahfrid here foreshadows that fifteenth-century scene which Shakespeare described; again roses are a sign of strife.

> A Holy Mary, Mother from whose womb was born the Son,
> Virgin of the purest faith, though bride in name of Joseph,
> O Bride and Queen and Dove, our Refuge and Friend for ever –
> pluck Thou Roses for war, for peace the smiling lily!
> To thee came a flower of the royal stem of Jesse,
> A single Son to restore the ancient line.
> By His holy word and life He sanctified the pleasant lily, dying
> He gave its colour to the rose.

This last line, it will be recalled, follows closely St Bernard:

Rosa passionis effusionibus crebis sacratissimi sanguinis sui specialites fuit rubricata.
(The effusion of His Sacred Blood has reddened the leaves of the Rose, bleeding for His sufferings.)

And the image continued to our own century in Plunkett's lines of 1916:

I see His blood upon the rose
And in the stars the glory of His eyes.

We have to wait several centuries after Walahfrid before a direct equation of the Virgin with the rose as *Flos florum*.

Authorship of the most elaborate of rose-symbolist poems, the *Roman de la Rose* is open to some doubt. It was probably begun by Guillaume de Lorris late in the thirteenth century. Also Thibaut le Chansonnier, who was so closely connected with the commercial cultivation of the Provins rose in the next century, may have had some hand in it. Geoffrey Chaucer's translation into English brought its fame from France.

The story is of the typical search for perfection which was the theme of courtly love that so obsessed the cultivated medieval mind. Here in the *Romaunt of the Rose* the troubadour – lover searches for, ostensibly, the perfect rosebud in a maze-like garden. It may be read at several levels. The search for the rose may be taken literally, the rose standing for an unattainable lover, or perhaps the whole poem is a satire upon contemporary *folies d'amour*. Whichever explanation or explanations we find personally acceptable, extracts from it bear repeating. If some of Chaucer's fourteenth-century words seem no longer current, to pronounce them phonetically is often effective (elumyned–illumined).

Toward the roser [rose bush] gan I go,
And whanne I was not far therefro,
The savour of the roses swote
Me swote right to the herte rote,
As I had al embalmed be.
And if I hadde endouted me [feared]
To have bin hated or assailed,
My thankis [willingly], wold I not have failed
To pull a rose of all that rout [number]
To beren in myn hande about,
And smellen to it where I wente;
But ever I dredde me to repent,
And lest it greved or forthought [displeased]
The lord that thilke garden wrought.
Of roses were ther grete wone [abundance],
So fair wax never ine rone [bush].
Of knoppes [buds] close some saw I there,
And some wel beter waxen were;
And some then ben of other moysoun [crop]
That drawe nigh to her [their] seasoun,
And sped hem faste for to sprede,

I love well siche roses rede;
For brode roses, and open also,
Ben passed in a day or two,
But knoppes willen freshe be
Two dayes atte least, or thre.
The knoppes gretely liked me,
For fairer may ther no man see.
Whoso might have one of all,
It ought him ben ful lief withal;
Might I garlond of hime getten,
For no richesse I wold it leten.

Fortunately, because roses are beautiful, not just as a concept, but in visible fact, poems which deal with them offer opportunities for illustration of which their contemporary painters have not failed to take advantage. Those accompanying editions of the *Romaunt of the Rose* are among the most evocative of early depictions of gardeners, gardens, and the plants, roses not excepted, that grew in them.

The conceit of the secret garden is a literary thread which can be traced from such medieval lyrics through, for example, Lewis Carroll and T. S. Eliot to the present day. Often, too, as with the *Romaunt* and *Alice*, the story is part of a dream sequence in which anything can, and frequently does, happen. In dreams, as we all know, the utterly desirable is at once more attainable yet ultimately always just out of reach.

This is, no doubt, part of the attraction of the rose-associated Mariolatry which combines the sacred and the secular. So much is there the general acceptance that Mary *is* (not just *like*) the *Flos florum* (the 'flower of flowers') that in many cases the actual statement is unspoken. But it is always assumed. Here, in an anonymous poem contemporary with the *Romaunt*, the Virgin is more than a rose flower; she is also a rose bush. This is the stock which acts as mankind's mediator with Heaven and his protection from Hell. Hence, 'Of a Rose is al Myn Song':

Of a rose, a lovely rose
Of a rose, a lovely rose
Of a rose is al myn song.

Lestynt lordynges, both elde and ynge,
How this rosë began to sprynge,
Swych a rosë to myn lykynge
In all this world ne knowe I non.

The aungil cam fro hevene tour,
To grete Marye with gret honour,
And seidë sche schuld bere the flour,
That schulde breke the fendes bond.
The flour sprong in heye Bedlem,
That is bothë bryght and schene,
The rose is Mary, hevenë quene,
Out of her bosum the blosme sprong.

The ferstë braunche is full of might,
That sprong on Crystemesse nyght;
The sterre schon over Bedlem bryght,
That is bothe brod and long.

The second braunche spring to helle,
The fendës power down to felle;
Therin myght non sowle dwelle
Blessed be the tyme the rose sprong.

The threddë braunche is good and swote,
Is sprong to hevenë crop and rote,
Therein to dwelle and ben our bote;
Every day it schewit in prestes hand.

Prey we to here with gret honour,
Sche that bare the blessid flour,
Sche be our helpe and our socour,
And schild us fro the fendës hand.

While the fourteenth-century language of such works prevents our immediate association with them and a gap of 500 years might seem an unbridgeable cultural chasm, this is not entirely so. Once a year as the Christmas season is celebrated, however materialistically, these words and concepts come round again in many of the carols we sing.

The fifteenth-century German words of '*Es ist ein' Ros' entsprungen'* are typical. This lovely carol appears in the *Speierschen Gesangbuch,* Cologne, dated 1600. Michael Praetorius composed the setting to which we sing 'A great and mighty wonder'.

J. M. Neale's adaptation begins:

A great and mighty wonder,
A full and blessed cure.
The Rose has come to blossom
which shall for ay endure.

But later versions omit all mention of the rose, so that the symbolism of the sixteenth-century German original is entirely lost. It may be that two of Neale's lines hold the key to this:

And idol forms shall perish
And error shall decay.

can be seen as mid-nineteenth-century Protestant bowdlerization. In other ways, however, attitudes both literary and religious had changed by that date.

A Protestant, post-Dissolution community in England especially brought other emphases to the fore. Queen Elizabeth I had, as has already been remarked, adopted (brazenly some thought) the Marian epithet of Virgin Queen and *Rosa sine spina* as a motto.

No doubt Sir John Davies's (1570–1626) clever piece of fulsome flattery was highly acceptable to Her Royal

Majesty (as was, on another day, Sir Walter Raleigh's cloak); its title may ostensibly offer it 'To the Rose,' but the initial letters of each line tell another story.

Eve of the golden, queene of flow'rs,
Love's cup wherein he nectar pours
Ingender'd first of nectar;
Sweet nurse-child of the spring's young houres,
And beautie's fair character.

Blest jewel that the earth doth wear,
E'en when the brave young sun draws near,
To her hot love pretending;
Himself likewise like form doth bear,
At rising and descending.

Rose of the Queen of Love belov'd
England's great Kings divinely mov'd
Gave Roses in their banner;
It showed that beautie's Rose indeed,
Now in this age should them succeed,
And reign in more sweet manner.

We see the late sixteenth and early seventeenth centuries as a golden age of elegant gallants who were often elegant versifiers as well. Rose imagery is constant. Where, before, the Marian symbolism led to roses until the person and the plant became interchangeable, the rose now developed its own anthropomorphism. Edmund Spenser (1552–1599) was a slightly earlier contemporary of Shakespeare's:

> Ah, see the virgin Rose, how sweetly she
> Doth first peep forth with bashful modesty,
> That fairer seems the less ye see her way!
> Lo! See soon after, how more bold and free,
> Her bared bosom she doth broad display:
> Lo! see soon after, how she fades away and falls.

Perhaps for one who enjoyed so sadly short a life as Spenser, it is apt that the continually encountered image of the rose epitomizing the ephemeral should be found in *The Faerie Queene*:

> So passeth in the passing of a day,
> Of mortal life the leaf, the bud, the flower
> No more doth flourish after first decay,
> That erst was sought to deck, both bed and bower,
> Of many a Lady, and many a Paramour;
> Gather therefore the Rose, while yet is prime,
> For soon comes age, that will her pride deflower:
> Gather the Rose of Love, whilst yet is time,
> Whilst loving thou mayst loved be with equal crime.

Robert Herrick, not much later, offers the same advice with more economy:

A romantic rose in the foreground of one of Walter Crane's illustrations to the Faerie Queene

Gather ye rosebuds while ye may,
Old time is still a-flying;
And this same flower that smiles today
Tomorrow will be dying.

Such sentiments are taken to extremes by Swinburne in his self-consciously alliterative lines:

Change in a trice
The Lilies and langours of virtue
For the raptures and roses of vice.

Ernest Dowson repeats the same image and introduces a further deathless phrase in his first line:

I have forgot much Cynara! gone with the wind,
Flung roses, roses, riotously with the throng,
Dancing to put thy pale, lost lilies out of mind.

Tennyson fortunately dispels at least something of thoughts that flowers might offer these alternatives with the question

And is there any moral shut
Within the bosom of the rose?

Any anthology of rose literature is bound to find Shakespeare bestriding, Colossus-like, Elizabethan and Jacobean verse. Roses are picked out to exemplify a season.

At Christmas I no more desire a rose
Than wish a snow in May's new-fangled mirth;
But like of each thing that in season grows.
(*Love's Labour Lost*)

Such a statement would have been applauded by the Stoic Seneca whose words (Epistle 22) are recalled:

> Live they not against nature that in winter long for a Rose, and by the nourishment of warm waters, and the first change of heat in winter time, cause a lily, a spring flower to bloom?

Roses are used to make more bitter the dynastic quarrels of Shakespeare's Tudor-partial histories, as has already been described in Chapter 2. But more telling and satisfying is the extended imagery devoted to the rose in Shakespeare's Sonnets: where two centuries earlier the rose was equated with the Queen of Heaven, here in sonnet 54, in a less overtly religious age, its equation is made directly with beauty.

> Oh how much more doth beautie beauteous seeme
> By that sweet ornament which truth doth give,
> The Rose lookes faire, but fairer we it deeme
> For that sweet odor, which doth in it live:
> The canker bloomes have full as deepe a die,
> As the perfumed tincture of the Roses,
> Hang on such thornes, and play as wantonly,
> When sommers breath their masked buds discloses:
> But for their virtue only is their show,
> They live unwoo'd and unrespected fade,
> Die to themselves. Sweet Roses doe not so,

Of their sweet deathes are sweetest odours made:
And so of you, beauteous and lovely youth,
When that shall fade, my verse distils your truth.

While such sophisticated artifice is one part of Shakespeare's art, that ability to evoke a scene with words alone is another. We do not need the professional stage designer's ideas to see the woodland glade in *A Midsummer Night's Dream* where, Puck says:

I know a bank whereon the wild thyme blows,
Where oxlips and the nodding violet grows
Quite over-canopied with luscious woodbine,
With sweet musk-roses, and with eglantine:
There sleeps Titania some time of the night,
Lull'd in these flowers with dances and delight;
And there the snake throws her enamell'd skin
Weed wide enough to wrape a fairy in.

In play after play the rose imagery appears, in the tragedies, the comedies and the histories, to symbolize or epitomize perfection.

Although relevant quotations from Shakespeare could continue for sometime (over sixty rose references have been noted) it is possible, and perhaps wise, to find lighter veins as the seventeenth century moves on. Henry Austin Dobson provides a suitably Restoration air, albeit in nineteenth-century pastiche:

The Ladies of St. James's!
They're painted to the eyes,
Their white it stays for ever,
Their red it never dies:
But Phyllida, my Phyllida,
Her colour comes and goes
It trembles to a lily, -
It wavers to a rose.

The lily/rose comparison appears almost too frequently in verse. The Knight at Arms who had so fraught a time with Keats's 'La Belle Dame Sans Merci' (inspired by the *Romaunt of the Rose*) is seen, it will be remembered, 'alone and palely loitering.' And then:

I see a lily on thy brow,
With anguish moist and fever dew;
And on thy cheek a fading rose
Fast withereth too.

In James Elroy Flecker's Arabian romance 'Hassan' these often paired flowers share the memorable lines:

How splendid in the morning flows the lily, with what grace he throws
His supplication to the rose.

Eglantine from Hortus Floridus *(1614-17)*

And we are thus brought close to Edward FitzGerald's realization of the *Rubaiyát of Omar Khayyám*, a Persian scholar, mathematician and scientist who died in AD 1123. This collection of four-line stanzas was brought together, translated and embellished by FitzGerald, from the original. Some of their mellifluous phrases have passed into our unconscious at a level of near-cliché.

The *Rubaiyát* offers a range of variations on the subject of human mutability, of resignation to the fact that youth ages and that memory fails. To this end the symbolism of flowers fading is admirably suited; no more so than when the chosen flower is itself symbolic of perfection. Although there is no continuous 'story,' two early stanzas prepare the atmosphere:

Come fill the cup, and in the Fire of Spring
The winter garment of Repentance fling:
The Bind of time has but a little way
To fly – and Lo! the bird is on the wing.
And look – a thousand Blossoms with the Day
Woke – and a thousand scatter'd into Clay:
And this first Summer Month that brings the Rose
Shall take Jamshyd and Kaikobád away.

One thing is certain that life flies
One thing is certain and the rest is lies
The Rose that once has blown forever dies.

Some of the stanzas are pure FitzGerald, even some which are best known and hence expected to be Omar:

I sometimes think that never blows so red
The Rose as where some buried Caesar bled;
That every Hyacinth the Garden wears
Dropt in its lap from some once lovely Head.

That roses should grow on graves appears one of the inevitabilities of poetry: verses of Thomas Hardy are used to illustrate this shortly. But with Omar, fact, poetry and legend here intermingle.

One of the poet's pupils, Khwajah Nizami of Samarkand, is recorded as saying:

> I often used to have conversations with my teacher Omar Khayyam, in a garden, and one day he said to me, 'My tomb shall be in a spot where the north wind may scatter roses over it.' I wondered at the words he spoke ... Years after, when I chanced to revisit Naishipur, I went to his final resting place and lo! it was just outside a garden, and trees laden with fruit stretched their boughs over the garden wall, and dropped their flowers upon his tomb, so that the stone was hidden under them.

It is apt therefore that a rose now bears his name; the story of its introduction is an interesting one.

Miss Ellen Willmott in *The Genus Rosa* (1912) records:

> A hip from a Rose planted on [Omar Khayyam's] grave at Naishipur was brought home by Mr Simpson, the artist of the *Illustrated London News*. It was given to me by the late Mr Bernard Quaritch, and reared at Kew. It proved to be *Rosa damascena*, and a shoot from the Kew plant has now been planted on the tomb of his first English translator, Edward FitzGerald.

The Kew Bulletin dates this: the hips were collected in 1884 and flowered at Kew a few years later.

'Omar Khayyam' is now available from the trade; an extremely prickly plant with deliciously scented pale pink flowers. The poet is worthily commemorated.

In the garden the rose is suggested as having, among other plants, a particular relationship with lilies: among animals its close associate is always the nightingale. To Katharine in *The Taming of the Shrew*:

> Say that she rail; why then I'll tell her plain
> She sings as sweetly as a nightingale:
> Say that she frown: I'll say she looks as clear
> As morning roses newly wash'd with dew.

And again with Omar:

> And David's lips are lockt; but in divine
> High-piping Pehlevi, with 'Wine! Wine! Wine!
> Red Wine!' – the nightingale cries to the Rose
> That sallow cheek of hers to incarnadine.

FitzGerald explains not very convincingly the obscurity of this in his notes to the first edition of 1859: 'I am not sure if this refers to the red rose looking sickly, or the yellow rose that ought to be red; red, white and yellow roses all common in Persia.' (Pehlevi was the old heroic Sanskrit of Persia in which the bird sang.)

Further legends cause the nightingale to make the rose red with her blood. In 'The Nightingale and the Rose'

The following pages show plates 19–22

Oscar Wilde tells an extraordinarily moving tale of self-sacrifice and ultimately of tragic waste.

In opera and ballet the rose is central in two works which are among the greatest of their form.

Le Spectre de la Rose is now the ballet by which Nijinsky is generally remembered. The scenario, after the Théophile Gautier poem, tells of a girl recalling her first ball, from which she has just returned. Tired but happy, she drifts off into sleep still holding the rose given to her by a favourite partner. At which the manifestation of the rose enters, waking the girl to dance with him in an ecstatic reincarnation of the happiness of the earlier ball.

In the original production Nijinsky' phenomenal leap from the room ended the piece: so often do roses epitomize compliant femininity, it is a surprise to find the embodied rose taking so athletically the opposite role.

Richard Strauss's *Rosenkavalier* is nearly contemporary with *Le Spectre*, having been first produced in Dresden in January 1911. The libretto by Hugo von Hoffmansthal is an elegant story of gallantry set in eighteenth-century Vienna. Sophie, the charming young daughter of a newly ennobled parvenu, is betrothed by her father to the bumpkin-baron, Ochs. It is the custom for a nobly born proxy to precede the first meeting with a gift of a silver rose to the bride-to-be from the prospective bridegroom.

Here the scene of the presentation of the rose, with the stand-in, young Oktavian, who has (of course) fallen immediately in love with Sophie, is one of the most exquisite in all opera. The young people are oblivious to the formal array of servants, soldiers, footmen and the fluttering of Sophie's duenna: the silver rose is central to the action. A memorable phrase from a recent poem by John Heath-Stubbs could describe it: 'In time of the unbearable tenderness of roses.' *Rosenkavalier* has much of that unbearable tenderness, to its protagonists and to the audience on the other side of the footlights.

Rose lyrics set to music offer further proof (if this be necessary) that the image appears in every past form, from early carols and hymns to the Virgin, to secular songs. Monteverdi's ravishing *Scherzi Musicali*, published in 1607, include:

> O Rosetta che rosetta
> Tra'l bel verde di tue frondi ...

'Pretty pink rose,' it runs in prosaic translation

> ... hiding among your leaves like a shy virgin, if I pick you I am sure you will not mind when I tell you what reward I expect for my pain. May you look even prettier in the hands of the lady who rules my thoughts, who looks into my heart and yet does not see my love for her.

There is less sophisticated imagery in two near-contemporary ballads from the early nineteenth century; but both are in the main stream of traditional rose-ness.

From Thomas Moore's *Irish Melodies:*

> This the last rose of summer
> Left blooming alone;
> All her lovely companions
> Are faded and gone.

And from Scotland Robert Burns:

> O my Luve's like a red red rose
> That's newly sprung in June;
> O my Luve's like the melodie
> That's sweetly play'd in tune.

The setting of Tennyson's poem 'Maud' is the archetypal Victorian drawing-room set-piece, difficult to sustain today without dissolving into irreverent mirth:

> Come into the garden, Maud
> For the black bat, night, has flown
> Come into the garden, Maud,
> I am here at the gate alone;
> And the woodbine spices are wafted abroad
> And the musk of the rose is blown.

By comparison, there is no difficulty in taking seriously William Blake's mystical verses, either as written or as sung to Benjamin Britten's haunting serenade for tenor and horn:

O rose, thou art sick!
The invisible worm,
That flies in the night,
In the howling storm,
Has found out thy bed
Of crimson joy,
And his dark secret love
Does thy life destroy.

The music here in Britten's setting is particularly ominous and seems to reflect Blake's vision of evil at the root of all things good. One of Shakespeare's sonnets explores the same ambiguity:

Roses have thorns, and silver fountains mud,
Clouds and eclipses stain both moon and sun,
And loathsome canker lives in sweetest bud,
As men make faults.

For the still darker side of rose-made poetry we come to our own century. Thomas Hardy's verse is so often based upon personal experience and person pain. The impact of the following verse was perhaps played down for publication (in 1920): in the manuscript version the first person pronoun is used throughout.

If you had known
You would lay roses,

Fifty years thence, on her monument, that discloses
Its greying shape upon the luxuriant green;
Fifty years thence to an hour, by chance led there,
What might have moved you? – yea, had you foreseen
That on the tomb of the selfsame one, gone where
The dawn of every day is as the close is,
You would lay roses!

Unhappiness, despair and imminent death are omnipresent factors of Hardy's vision of the human condition. Yet in 'Transformations' man's essential oneness with all living organisms, even if only as decayed matter, emerges: it is, of course another graveyard scene.

Portion of this yew
Is a man my grandsire knew,
Bosomed here at its foot:
This branch may be his wife
A ruddy human life
Was turned to a green shoot.

These grasses must be made
Of her who often prayed,
Last century, for repose;
And the fair girl, long ago
Whom I often tried to know
Maybe entering this rose.

So, they are not underground,
But as nerves and veins abound
In the growths of upper air,
And they feel the sun and rain,
And the energy again
That made them what they were!

For W. B. Yeats, too, the rose had a highly symbolic significance, as seen in such poems as 'The Rose of Peace', 'The Rose of Battle' and 'To the Rose upon the Rood of Time' and it is often invested with his marvellous and mysterious sonority:

Far off, most secret and inviolate Rose
Enfold me in my hour of hours.

His countryman, James Joyce, produced for *Pomes Penyeach* two simple and poignant verses that need no commentary.

A Flower given to My Daughter
Frail the white rose and frail are
Her hands that gave
Whose soul is sere and paler
Than time's wan wave.
Rose frail and fair – yet frailest
A wonder wild
In gentle eyes thou veilest,
My blueveined child.

In the pantheon of great twentieth-century poets, T. S. Eliot is bound to take a foremost place. Here one can only touch on his complex use of rose imagery. The *Four Quartets* appear at first approachable through the images of the English countryside. The first of the four poems, 'Burnt Norton,' evokes the medieval enclosed garden-paradise.

> Footfalls echo in the memory
> Down the passage which we did not take
> Towards the door we never opened
> Into the rose-garden
>   …for the roses
> Had the look of flowers that are looked at.

Roses appear, too, in 'East Coker' and 'The Dry Salvages', other poems in the *Quartets*; only careful reading, however, will unfold Eliot's layers of meaning about the earthly condition of man. We may not like what we find.

In the last of the *Four Quartets*, 'Little Gidding', the concern continues with the fleetingness of man's life and his possessions; the rose becomes symbolic of memory, of the best of things past.

> Ash on an old man's sleeve
> Is all the ash the burnt roses leave.
> Dust in the air suspended
> Marks the place where a story ended.

Dust inbreathed was a house –
The wall, the wainscot and the mouse.
The death of hope and despair,
    This is the death of air.

It also represents an image of passionate sensuality which must be reconciled with the spiritual liberation of the senses:

And all shall be well and
All manner of thing shall be well
When the tongues of flame are in-folded
Into the crowned knot of fire
And fire and the rose are one.

This final reference to the rose draws heavily on traditional Christian symbolism and thus, most fittingly, T. S. Eliot and the *Four Quartets* take us back to the beginnings of rose imagery.

Fortunately not all of it is so demanding upon the intellect, though. As Alice found when at last she managed to get into the garden, things can be highly confusing and not always what they seem:

> A large rose-tree stood near the entrance of the garden: the roses growing on it were white, but there were three gardeners at it, busily painting them red. Alice thought this a very curious thing, and she went nearer to watch

> them, and just as she came up to them, she heard one of them say 'Look out now, Five! Don't go splashing paint over me like that!'
>
> 'Would you tell me, please,' said Alice, a little timidly, 'Why are you painting those roses?' Five and Seven said nothing, but looked at Two. Two began in a low voice 'Why the fact is, you see, Miss, this here ought to have been a *red* rose-tree; and we put a white one in by mistake; and, if the Queen was to find out, we should all have our heads cut off, you know. So you see, Miss, we're doing our best afore she comes to- .' At this moment, Five, who had been anxiously looking across the garden, called out 'The Queen! The Queen!' and the three gardeners instantly threw themselves flat upon their faces. There was a sound of many footsteps, and Alice looked round, eager to see the Queen.

But at least in *Wonderland* the flowers keep themselves to themselves. In *Through the Looking-Glass* the situation is very different. Alice made the mistake, in her confusion to find the right way of saying to a Tiger-lily:

> … that was waving gracefully about in the wind, 'I wish you could talk!'
>
> 'We can talk' said the Tiger-lily: 'when there is anybody worth talking to.'

Such acid remarks are typical of the flowers there.

> 'It is *my* opinion that you never think *at all*,' the Rose said in a rather severe tone.
> 'I never saw anybody that looked stupider,' a Violet said, so suddenly, that Alice quite jumped, for it hadn't spoken before.
> 'Hold *your* tongue!' cried the Tiger-lily, 'As if *you* ever saw anybody! You keep your head under the leaves and snore away there, till you know no more what's going on in the world, than if you were a bud!'
> 'Are there any more people in the garden besides me?' Alice said, not choosing to notice the Rose's last remark.

And enter the Red Queen.

The possession of human attributes is not bestowed upon roses by Lewis Carroll only. Speaking roses are relatively common, but they usually do it in verse. Thomas Hardy provides a good example in 'The Fading Rose':

> I saw a rose, in bloom, but sad,
> Shedding the petals that still it had
> And I heard it say: 'O where is she
> Who used to come and muse on me?'

Roses not only talk but, like walls, have ears.

> All night have the roses heard
> The flute, violin, bassoon.

And eyes, if Sheridan's charming invitation to a pretty girl is to be taken literally.

> Won't you come into the garden? I would like my roses
> to see you.

Poets seldom seem to differentiate, except in colour where white and red have their own roles, between types of roses, which, as we have seen, are legion. Not all writers have been as undiscerning as Gertrude Stein in her oft-quoted circular 'Rose is a Rose is a Rose'. Shelley, for example, in 'The Sensitive Plant', is conscious of the highly double Centifolias and Gallicas of his time:

> And the rose like a nymph to the bath addressed,
> Which unveiled the depth of her glowing breast
> Till, fold after fold, to the fainting air
> The soul of her beauty and love lay bare.

And on the way to The Old Vicarage, Grantchester, Rupert Brooke is equally clear about the single-flowered wild species of the roadside.

> There the dews
> Are soft beneath a moon of gold
> Here tulips bloom as they are told:
> Unkempt about those hedges blows
> An English unofficial rose.

In spite of much elegant lip-service to flowers, versifiers seem to have little inclination for actually becoming involved with the growing of the plants they eulogize, Vita Sackville-West being an obvious exception.

A more surprising rose gardener was Edward Lear – he of the exquisite topographical paintings and the Nonsense Botany. Toward the end of his life he lived near San Remo and took more and more practical delight in his garden: 'Can you fancy me,' he writes to a correspondent, 'overseeing fences and a cistern, digging a terrace, and planting beans – making blinds and picking olives? – yet such is my occupation in these late days.'

Enthusiasm for roses ('I think I prefer Climbers to all other plants – they are so obligingly given to save space by growing perpendicular') has seldom been so happily expressed:

And this is certain, if so be
You could just now my garden see,
The aspic of my flowers so bright
Would make you shudder with delight.

And if you voz to see my roziz
As is a boon to all men's noziz, -
You'd fall upon your back and scream –
'O Lawk, O Crikey! It's a dream!'

CHAPTER 9

THE MAKING OF 'PEACE': THE BIOGRAPHY OF A ROSE

A modern rose bears visible traces of its earlier forms. Gradual selection of desirable forms of wild species and natural hybrids, careful subsequent cross-breeding and rigorous rogueing of seedlings combine, layer upon layer, to make a flower our ancestors could never have known.

Any one of hundreds of cultivars currently offered could be chosen as the subject of such a biography but it needs to be one which is distinctive and loved by all. Amazingly, to those of us who remember it bursting upon a war-weary world, the rose selected is now nearly seventy-five years old. It is admirably named: 'Peace'.

The distinction of 'Peace' is startlingly obvious: great glossy leaves and massive growths build up fine flowers of enormous size. In colour they are basically a pale, clear yellow with pink tints towards the edge of the petals and, as the open flower ages, this pink is gradually suffused through the yellow, like the light of dawn replacing the moon. Its scent is light and fresh. Perhaps no rose has enjoyed such rapid and lasting popularity, perhaps none has so deserved it.

As a classic modern Hybrid Tea, 'Peace' can trace back its family tree through members of its class for almost 100 years, through earlier Hybrid Perpetuals to roses grown by the Empress Josephine at Malmaison. These in turn hold threads, like that unwound by Ariadne in the Palace of the Minotaur, which link 'Peace' with at least six wild roses. Unfortunately, for the full success of the maze analogy, the famous Rose of Knossos is not among them; yet the story is sufficiently labyrinthine to make it apt.

The story spreads across the old world from the shores of the Mediterranean in the west to China in the east, into Asia Minor between these geographical extremes as the initial melting pot. Although over 100 wild species of rose are to be found in the northern hemisphere (none naturally cross the equator) only a few of these have been used in the parentage of modern roses. All the important ones are represented in 'Peace'.

The early combinations begin with those roses of the classical world which provided cut-flowers for Egyptian and Roman feasts. *R. gallica*, known as the French or Provence rose, is central. Combined with the Phoenician rose (or some similar species – for much of the early family tree of 'Peace,' like that of any blue-blooded aristocrat, is necessarily speculative) it made the Summer Damask rose; and with the Musk rose it made the Autumn Damask.

These three species and their immediate offspring produced during a couple of thousand years or so a considerable number of forms. These comprise most of the pre-nineteenth-century garden roses. It needed voyages of discovery and knowledge of plant sexuality for keen gardeners to develop roses further. These desiderata were combined when, in the 1790s, the first China roses were brought from that country to western Europe. Already these were garden plants of some antiquity which existed in several varieties.

With the Summer Damask rose, Slater's Crimson China began a group known as Portland roses. Parson's Pink China combined with the Autumn Damask and led to the Bourbons. *R. gallica* itself was crossed with Hume's Blush Tea-scented China to produce in 1815 the first Hybrid Chinas.

Hume's variety itself was only half a China. Its other parent was the giant wild Tea rose: perhaps a distant gene from this extravagantly vigorous climber emerged to give 'Peace' its strength. The Hume's variety was in turn crossed with the Bourbons, while the Hybrid Chinas became allied to the Portlands. These two liaisons gave rise to pink Tea roses and to Hybrid Perpetuals.

Thus, by the 1830s, five ancestral rose species and their various interlocking hybrids had produced hundreds of rose varieties which embellished the gardens, especially in France, of a public which was rapidly becoming rose-conscious. Variations in shape, texture, remontancy and scent were great. Colour also knew its variations but within a band we would now consider more than a little restricted. There were no yellow garden roses.

At last, in 1900, a sixth species was added to this complicated genetic stew: a Hybrid Perpetual was crossed with the Austrian Copper (*R. foetida bicolor*) and 'Soleil d'Or' was born. Meanwhile the pink Tea roses had also been added to some Perpetuals to begin that race, the Hybrid Teas, which dominated the twentieth-century. Some old cultivars in the ancestry of 'Peace' are still famous and still grown. 'Mme Caroline Testout' is a vigorous rose – satin pink though without much scent. Twenty years younger, 'Ophelia' is a delicate pink with blush and cream tones: it is highly fragrant and of excellent form.

So far so clear to this grandparental point but now follows two generations crossing unnamed seedlings that those grandparents had produced and M Meilland's records vary somewhat. Perhaps a little blip in such a family tree doesn't matter.

In the Meilland trial grounds in 1939, this rose, still unnamed, attracted great admiration and, now that its quality was clear, buds were sent to the raisers' distributors in Germany, Italy and the United States to build up stocks for retail sale. But in September Europe was plunged into war and communications soon ceased between France and those countries – a sad comparison with the situation 140 years earlier when, at the height of the Napoleonic Wars, the British Navy had orders positively to expedite the shipment of roses to the Empress Josephine, blockade or no.

In the less gallant 1940s the nurseries in each country which were growing this particular rose introduced it without reference to the raiser. In Germany it was named 'Gloria Dei,' in Italy 'Giola' and in France, its legitimate home, it became 'Mme A. Meilland.'

In the United States the Conard-Pyle Company had been particularly successful with this already, unknown to them, three-named rose. 1945 was an auspicious year, marking the end of the war, and at a ceremony on 29 April, under the auspices of the American Rose Society, the rose at last got the famous and significant name by which it has become known throughout the English-speaking world.

2 *Rosa rubra.*
The red Rose.

3 *Rosa Prouincialis, siue Damascena.*
The Prouince, or Damaske Rose.

Appendix

Rosaceae AND *Rosa* AS FAMILY AND GENUS

In the simple pre-Darwinian world it was confidently stated that the Creation occurred in the year 4004 BC and it was thought only a matter of time before man would be able to make a full tally of the world's plant resources. After all, they had been put there by a beneficent deity who, as Hooker and Arnott (both eminent botanists) confidently wrote in their *Flora* of 1860, had 'simultaneously called them into existence on the third day of creation each distinct from the other and destined to remain so'. As such there was a finite number, countable.

Unfortunately for Hooker and Arnott things do not stand still. Species do change, particularly by mutation and natural selection, to the point at which the fittest and most able survive. Over evolutionary time the higher plants have produced possibly 300,000 or so true-breeding species in the world today. How many have been lost on the way in the fight for survival will never be known. Indeed, in the rapidly declining areas of tropical rainforest are many species still unknown, perhaps of great beauty or of economic importance, that will be lost to the world in our own lifetime. It is believed that one disappears every day and extinction is extraordinarily permanent.

The higher plants as we know them, in all their amazing diversity, from tiny alpine cushions to giant eucalypts 400 feet high, from ephemeral annuals which rush through their life cycle of germination back to seed again, to forest giants which measure their life-span in centuries, are the product of perhaps the last 150 million years. The earliest angiosperms, the flowering plants, seem to have appeared toward the end of the Jurassic period, itself two billion years on from the projected time at which life on this plant recognizably began in the form of bacteria and blue-green algae.

Although many of the earliest flowering plants no longer exist, evolution, of course, does not necessarily mean that in the development of new forms all old ones become extinct. It may be that hitherto-unused habitats, or what are often referred to as 'ecological niches,' became colonized by the new development, leaving the progenitors behind where they were already dominant. Hence plant life today contains species of every evolutionary period from the truly ancient to those of the present. The time-span of man's recorded history is so short in these terms that it is not easy to accept evolution as a continuous process of which all organisms, animal and plant, are fully paid-up members.

While different authorities offer different sequences of evolutionary development, certain higher plants' families are usually regarded as 'primitive', while others are considered highly developed. There is some general agreement at the beginning and end of the list but a certain amount of shuffling about between the extremes is common as further evidence from fossil deposits or pollen records is gathered, and as the relatively new science of cytology (plant genetics) is brought to bear upon the problems of taxonomy (principles of classification).

The main diversion of the higher plants is accepted by all botanists: that into dicotyledons and monocotyledons. It is also easily accepted and recognized by the layman. A cotyledon is a seed-leaf and if one sows seeds of radish, runner bean, rose or rhododendron what emerges first (if the sowing fingers were green enough) is a pair of cotyledons on a stem with a tiny bud in between. On the other hand, seeds of grasses, sedges, lilies and irises produce just one seed-leaf.

This main divide continues to be obvious in most plants into maturity: the broad leaves with netted veins of the dicots and the long, narrow, parallel-veined leaves of the monocots. This latter group is usually considered to be the more advanced, having broken away from the dicots at a very early stage.

Both groups then can be said to have originated from primitive flowering plants, known as protoangiosperms, which no longer exist, and have developed their amazing diversity in response to climate, soil, altitude, exposure and all the variations of habitat they have experienced over at least 150 million years. For classificatory convenience plants are further divided into subdivisions, orders, tribes and families. Although authorities tend to differ we find toward the start of any description an evolutionary progression to well-known families. These are the *Magnoliaceae* and the *Ranunculaceae* (a family name is coined by adding the *aceae* suffix to the generic name of the plant considered to be the most typical in the group). The order (*Ranales*) which contains both these families and several others with primitive characters is linked immediately by most authorities with the *Rosales*. This includes the two dicot families of the greatest importance to man, *Rosaceae* and *Leguminosae*.

The more advanced of the two, *Leguminosae* (an old name referring to its typical 'legume' or pod) is the pea family which provides food for people (peas, beans, peanuts, soya, lentils), fodder for stock (clover, alfalfa, vetches) and ornamentals for gardens (lupin, mimosa, sweet pea) as well as timber, dyestuffs and fibres. With at least 13,000 species, the *Leguminosae* is one of the biggest plant families. *Orchidaceae* and *Compositae* are even more extensive, but the legumes are more widely distributed and of far greater economic importance. The *Leguminosae's* immediate precursor is *Rosaceae*, equally packed with plants that man has made his own. These include almost all the tree-fruits grown in the temperate world, such as apples, pear, plum, quince, cherry, prune, peach, medlar, loquat, nectarine, apricot. There are soft fruits: blackberry, raspberry, strawberry and many ornamentals giving flower or fruit.

Altogether the *Rosaceae* contains around ninety genera and well over 2,000 species from all over the world with the three main centres of distribution being Eastern Asia, including China and the Himalayas, North American and Europe. About fifty genera are native to the United States; there are thirty-four in Europe of which all but ten are also found wild in the British Isles, an indication of the family's preference for a cool temperate life.

The biggest collections of species occur in the genera *Potentilla* (300+), *Rubus* (approximately 750), *Crataegus* (approximately 500), *Prunus* (approximately 175) and Rosa (approximately 150), although some authorities suggest more. In spite of these considerable numbers and the fact that they encompass great diversity of form, *Rosaceae* is a very 'natural' family – that is, it holds together as a group without any great effort of imagination or wilful manipulation by the observing botanist. Even laymen are usually able to recognize its members: any immediate confusion with the *Ranunculaceae* is clarified by observing rosaceous stipules (small leaf-like growths at the base of the leaf-stalk).

Rosaceae, as has become obvious, contains trees, shrubs and herbaceous plants with usually alternate leaves and bisexual flowers. Sepals and petals are basically in rings of five with many stamens normally surrounding the stigmas. The arrangements of these floral parts and the ways in which the fruits are subsequently formed from them are used to group the genera into six tribes or subfamilies.

The rose family is broad indeed, with wide differences of habit, perennation method and distribution. But obviously the similarities must exceed the differences for such diversity to be brought together in a number of genera to constitute the family. It is the floral structure which epitomizes these similarities.

This brings us back to look more closely at the type-genus, *Rosa*. Recognizable roses have been discovered from fossil deposits in Colorado and Oregon in the south-western United States. These date from some 32 million years ago and, though these records are perhaps less than a third of the age of the first roses, it is comforting to have tangible proof that roses have been part of the earth's flora for so long.

What has been maintained is the basic floral symmetry, most primitively retained in *Spiraea* but much more easily seen in *Rosa* itself. Throughout its 150 or so wild species (see Chapter 3), the floral pattern is generally constant. Above a shrubby base, often scrambling to considerable heights, flowers are carried singly or in heads. The pattern is pentamerous with five sepals, sometimes spreading and almost leafy, supporting five petals. Within is the boss of yellow, pollen-bearing stamens surrounding centrally a number of pollen-receptive styles.

The flowers are also homogenous, that is with stamens and stigmas becoming ripe at the same time. Few roses possess nectar as an attractant to insects, so these visit the flowers for pollen – the mass of stamens make this both worthwhile for the bee and dispensable for the flower. Scent floating in the air of course acts in conjunction with the colourful petals to encourage visitation. If, however, through bad weather or some other misfortune, insects fail to effect transfer of pollen (hopefully from another flower of the same species, from stamen to stigma) then self-pollination is possible. It is this accommodating facility, though ultimately undesirable if continued for generations, which so many cultivated rosaceous top fruit varieties lack; thus the gardener has to ensure that compatible pollen is available from another tree if good crops of fruit are to be picked.

Although the roles of the floral parts are similar for all the species of rose, the variation in colour, size, presence and absence of scent, time of flowering and length of season relate to the conditions to which each species – whether a great Himalayan climber of a dwarf bush of Scottish sea-shore sands – have become adapted through evolution. These variations are their marks of success.

Some appear of little importance to the plant, yet such has been the interest in roses, long before the development of modern scientific botany, that observations have been made and note taken. One such example refers to the so-called aestivation, that is, the way in which the sepals and petals are arranged in the unopened bud, of *R. canina* and other dog roses. It is explained by Professor W. T. Stearn in the title 'The Five brethren of the rose: an old botanical riddle'.[1] There are several versions in Latin of this medieval verse. One runs:

Qunique sumus fratres, et eodem tempore nati
Sunt duo barbati, duo sunt barba absque creati
Unus et e quinque non est barbatus utrinque
In a summer's day, in sultry weather
Five brethren were born together
Two had beards and two had none
And the other had half a one.

It is not known where the riddle originated or who made the first observation that provoked it but it has an oral tradition going back to the twelfth century AD. The reference, obscure to the uninstructed, is to the arrangement of the dog-rose calyx by which the outside edges of the sepals surround the bud in a fringed beard.

Instead of a cyclic overlapping of the five members, two sepals have both edges tucked in while two others are fully out. The fifth has one edge in and one out. Thus all outside edges have these outgrowths to make up two bearded brothers, two bald brothers and one who appears to have been disturbed at shaving time!

The arrangement of bearded and beardless sepals and how they overlap

Sir Thomas Browne, English essayist of the seventeenth century, writes about the phenomenon in detail:

> Nothing is more admired than the five brethren of the Rose, and the strange disposure of the appendices or beards on the calycular leaves thereof … For those two which are smooth and of no beard are contrived to be undermost, as without prominent parts, and fit to be smoothly covered, the other two which are beset with beards on either side stand outwards and uncovered, but the fifth or half-bearded leaf is covered on the one side, but on the open side stands free and bearded like the other.

Careful medieval observation added to the body of knowledge accumulated about the rose. At the other extreme only modern microscopy could have brought the new science of cytology to bear. The Moravian monk Gregor Mendel demonstrated in the 1870s that there were heritable characteristics in plants (and hence by inference in all living things) which were passed from one generation to the next. Working especially with garden peas, he showed that some characters were dominant while others lay dormant (recessive) for one or more generations. Predictions could be made about their reappearance. Later work, built upon what was afterward called Mendelism, showed that all living body cells of an organism carry the full complement of these factors which made it the species, plant or animal that it is.

Observation under a high-powered microscope of cell nuclei at certain stages of their development shows thread-like structures with swellings along their length, the whole resembling a necklace of beads. These are chromosomes, the 'beads' being the genes, each of which is responsible for a characteristic of the species. This is not to say that any one gene is only responsible for, say, bristly stems or red flowers; it may have several roles, but without its presence bristly stems or red flowers will not occur. Growth of living organisms is not by any form of elastic-like extension but by constant division of the cells. Every cell division implies exact replication of the cell, including, naturally, the nucleus, its chromosomes and its genes. Thus the new cell maintains the genetic complement of the species.

Chromosome numbers are constant within a true-breeding wild species and are usually given as the diploid number because that is how they exist in every normal body cell of the plant. Thus the Sweet Pea diploid chromosome number is 14 and written 2n=14, peach and redcurrant 2n=16, wild lettuce 2n=18, Man 2n=46. It is shown thus because every plant or animal which is produced by a sexual method of reproduction has within its cells a double set of chromosomes, built up from each parent. In plants, what we call fertilization is the union of the egg cell with the germ cells carried by male pollen. Obviously, if every female egg cell and male germ cell carried the number of chromosomes of the body cells of the plant to which they belonged, the chromosome complement would double at each generation. This clearly would not work and a method by which the chromosome number is reduced by a half at sexual-cell production has been evolved. It is known technically as meiosis or reduction division. During the formation of germ cells the nucleus divides rapidly twice while the chromosomes only do so once. Tetrads of four daughter nuclei are formed, each with a haploid number of chromosomes. When these fuse at fertilization with a cell of the opposite sex and their chromosomes pair, the body-cell diploid number is regained and maintained in cell-division as the embryo develops into dormant seed, seed into germinated seedling and seedling into mature plant.

In the genus *Rosa* the chromosome number is almost invariably in multiples of seven, this being the haploid or half-diploid number which exists, as just indicated, at the reduction division stage. Any number above the typical diploid number is described as being polyploid. Among wild roses *R. rugosa* has the basic dipolid number of chromosomes, the Scots Burnet is tetraploid with double that number and the European dog-rose is pentaploid with thirty-five. From further afield come the triploid *R. woodsii* (twenty-one), the hexaploid *R. moyesii* (forty-two) and the octoploid *R. hilliana* (fifty-six).

Reasons for the phenomenon of polyploidy are diverse, one of them being a suppression of the reduction division so that sexual cells emerge from meiosis with a full body-cell number. If one of these fertilizes a normal sexual cell, the diploid of the one combining with the haploid of the other produces a triploid offspring. Such plants are likely to be sterile, especially as odd, unpaired, chromosomes occur at their meiosis stage.

Polyploid numbers can, however, indicate earlier forms from which some chromosomes have been lost over evolutionary time. There has been a suggestion[2] that a northern decaploid species was the initial ancestral rose, now extinct, from which currently existing species have been derived through chromosomal loss. As it is assumed that loss is easier and hence a more usual mutation than the obtaining of new chromosomes, the suggestion is quite feasible.

The important point to emphasize in any basic outline of the genetics of roses is that a wide chromosome number makes, at one level, for the possibility of great hybrid variation (indeed some apparently good species are most probably originally of hybrid background) and at another time for the production of sterile types that have little normal hope of reproduction. They have arrived, it might be said, at the end of their particular road. As Ann P. Wylie stated in her Masters' Memorial Lectures to the Royal Horticultural Society, London, in 1966:

> Although there are many polypoid rose species, these are found principally in the sections which have not contributed to garden rose development. Of the important ancestors, *R. gallica* (and its derivatives) and *R. foetida* are tetraploids, while all the rest are diploids.

The 'sections' to which reference is made are those into which the American botanist Rehder grouped the species *Rosa* in 1940. This arrangement is generally accepted and mentioned in most texts. Rehder proposed four subgenera which need not concern us here except to relate that one includes all the roses as we know them, the other three are very small and until very recently had no expectation of affecting rose breeding. At last, however

Hulthemia (or *Rosa*) *persica* has been grown successfully enough to do so.

In the main group (which Rehder calls *Eurosa*) there are ten sections. These are shown in the following list (see right), where it can be quickly seen which species have had considerable effect upon our garden roses, which have made some contribution, and which wild species from all over the world are grown in gardens for their natural beauty of flower, foliage or fruit – or as with the delightful *R. glauca (rubrifolia)*, for all three. Clearly, visual differences between the sections are several. The *synstylae*, as the name suggests, have fused styles which protrude from the receptacle (that part of the flower on which the sexual parts stand): the same protrusion occurs in *R. chinensis* but here the styles are free or separate. The other sections are short-styled, varying in inflorescence type and in other ways. It will be noted that the diagram lists seem to omit certain apparently obvious names. But these, such as *R. centifolia* and *R. alba,* are in fact historic hybrids.

[1] *Huntia,* 2, pp. 180–184, 1965.

[2] R. E. Shepherd, *The History of the Rose*, 1954.

Sections: *Cinnamomeae* and *Carolinae* (diploid to octoploid)
48 species: *rugosa, cinnamomea*

Section: *Synstylae* (diploid)
23 species: ***multiflora, wichuraiana, moschata***, *phoenicia, sempervirens, arvensis, filipes, longicuspis*

Section: *Caninae* (tetraploid to hexaploid)
23 species: *rubiginosa*

Section: *Pimpinellifoliae* (diploid and hexaploid)
10 species: ***foetida***, *spinosissima*

Section: *Gallicanae* (tetraploid)
4 species: ***gallica***, ***damascena***

Section: *Indicae* (diploid)
3 species: ***chinensis***, ***gigantea***

Section: *Banksianae* (diploid)
2 species: *banksiae*

Section: *Bracteatae* (diploid)
2 species: *bracteata*

Section: *Laevigatae* (diploid)
1 species: *laevigata*

The above shows the number of species in each section. Those in ***bold type*** have made an important contribution; those in *italics* are less significant in breeding; *italics and underlined* shows the wild roses commonly grown in gardens

Select Bibliography

American Rose Annual, 1917 *et seq.*

Amherst, Alicia, *A History of Gardening in England*, 1896

Andrews, H. C., *Roses: a monograph of the Genus Rosa*, 2 vols, 1805-28

Blackwell, Elizabeth, *A Curious Herbal*, 1737-1782

Bowles, E. A., *My Garden in Summer*, 1914

Bunyard, Edward., *Old Garden Roses*, 1936

Burnett, M. A., *Plantae utilitores*, 1847

Cochet-Cochet, P. C. M. and Mottet, S., *Les Rosiers*, 1896 *et seq.*

Curtis, Henry, *Beauties of the Rose*, 1850-53

Curtis, W., *Flora Londinensis*, 1777-98

— (ed), *Botanical Magazine*, 1787 *et seq.*

D'Ombrain, Henry H. (ed), *The Rosarian's Year Book*, 1877-1902

Ellacombe, Henry N., *In a Gloucestershire Garden*, 1895

Fostar-Melliar, Andrew, *The Book of the Rose*, 1919

Gardener's Chronicle, 1814 *et seq.*

Gault, S. Millar and Synge, Patrick M., *The Dictionary of Roses in Colour*, 1971

Gerard, John, *The Herball,* 1597
Gibson, Michael, *The Book of the Rose,* 1980
Gravereaux, Jules, *Les Roses,* 1912
Harkness, John, *Roses*, 1978
Hariot, Paul, *Le Livre d'Or des Roses,* 1904
Harvey, N. P., *The Rose in Britain*, 1951
Hole, Dean S. Reynolds, *A Book about Roses,* 1870
Hollis, L., *Roses,* 1974
Hurst, Dr C. C. in *The Old Shrub Roses* by G. S. Thomas, 1955
Jamain, Hippolyte and Fourney, Eugene, *Les Roses,* 1893
Jekyll, Gertrude and Mawley, Edward, *Roses for English Gardens,* 1902
Journal des Roses, 1877-1914
Keays, Mrs Frederick Love, *Old Roses,* 1935
Kordes, Wilhelm, *Rosen,* 1932
Lawrence, Mary, *A Collection of Roses from Nature,* 1799
Lindley, John, *Rosarium Monographia,* 1820
L'Obel, M. de, *Plantarum seu stirpium icones,* 1581
MacSelf, A. J., *The Rose Growers' Treasury,* 1934
— *Modern Roses III,* 1947
McFadden, Dorothy Loa, *Touring the Gardens of Europe,* 1965
McFarland, J. Horace, *The Rose in America*, 1926
Miller, Philip, *The Gardener's Dictionary,* 1731-68
National Rose Society Annuals, 1907 *et seq.*
Nicolas, J. H., *The Rose Odyssey,* 1937
Parkinson, John, *Paradisi in Sole, Paradisus Terrestris,* 1629
— *Theatrum Botanicum,* 1640
Parsons, Samuel B., *The Rose,* 1847
Passe, Crispin van der the Younger, *Hortus Floridus,* 1614-17
Paul, William, *The Rose Garden,* 1848, 1872 *et seq.*
Pemberton, Reverend Joseph H., *Roses: their History Development and Cultivation,* 1908

Redouté, P-J, *Les Roses,* 1817-24
Rehder, Alfred, *Manual of Cultivated Trees and Shrubs,* 1947
Robinson, W., *The English Flower Garden,* 1883
Roessig, D., *Les Roses,* 1802-20
Thomas, G. S., *The Old Shrub Roses* (revised edn.), 1961
— *Shrub Roses of Today,* 1962
— Climbing Roses Old and New (revised edn.), 1978
Turner, W., *A New Herbal,* 1568
Vibert, P-J, *Essai sur les roses,* 1824
Willmott, E. A., *The Genus Rosa,* 1910-14
Wylie, A. P. in *Journal of the Royal Horticultural Society,* vol LXXIX,
p. 555, December 1954
— The History of Garden Roses, *Endeavour,* vol. XIV, 56, October 1955

Indexes

General Index

Index of Roses by Common and Cultivar Name

Index of Roses by Botanical Name